A COLLECTION OF ESSAYS ON

SPIRITUALISM

BY

ALFRED RUSSEL WALLACE

British Library Cataloguing-in-Publication Data
A catalogue record for this book is available from the
British Library

CONTENTS

CONTENTS

Alfred Russel Wallace

Alfred Russel Wallace was born on 8th January 1823 in the village of Llanbadoc, in Monmouthshire, Wales.

At the age of five, Wallace's family moved to Hertford where he later enrolled at Hertford Grammar School. He was educated there until financial difficulties forced his family to withdraw him in 1836. He then boarded with his older brother John before becoming an apprentice to his eldest brother, William, a surveyor. He worked for William for six years until the business declined due to difficult economic conditions.

After a brief period of unemployment, he was hired as a master at the Collegiate School in Leicester to teach drawing, map-making, and surveying. During this time he met the entomologist Henry Bates who inspired Wallace to begin collecting insects. He and bates continued exchanging letters after Wallace left teaching to pursue his surveying career. They corresponded on prominent works of the time such as Charles Darwin's *The Voyage of the Beagle* (1839) and Robert Chamber's *Vestiges of the Natural History of Creation* (1844).

Wallace was inspired by the travelling naturalists of the day and decided to begin his exploration career collecting specimens in the Amazon rainforest. He explored the Rio Negra for four years, making notes on the peoples and languages he encountered as well as the geography, flora, and fauna. On his return voyage his ship, Helen, caught fire and he and the crew were stranded for ten days before being picked up by the Jordeson, a brig travelling from Cuba to London. All of his specimens aboard Helen had been lost.

After a brief stay in England he embarked on a journey to the Malay Archipelago (now Singapore, Malaysia, and Indonesia). During this eight year period he collected more than 126,000 specimens, several thousand of which represented new species to science. While travelling, Wallace refined his thoughts about evolution and in 1858 he outlined his theory of natural selection in an article he sent to Charles Darwin. This was published in the same year along with Darwin's own theory. Wallace eventually published an account of his travels *The Malay Archipelago* in 1869, and it became one of the most popular books of scientific exploration in the 19th century.

Upon his return to England, in 1862, Wallace became a staunch defender of Darwin's landmark work *On the Origin of Species* (1859). He wrote responses to those critical of the theory of natural selection, including 'Remarks on the Rev. S. Haughton's Paper on the Bee's Cell, And on the Origin of Species' (1863) and 'Creation by Law' (1867). The former of these was particularly pleasing to Darwin. Wallace also published important papers such as 'The Origin of Human Races and the Antiquity of Man Deduced from the Theory of 'Natural Selection" (1864) and books, including the much cited *Darwinism* (1889).

Wallace made a huge contribution to the natural sciences and he will continue to be remembered as one of the key figures in the development of evolutionary theory.

Wallace died on 7th November 1913 at the age of 90. He is buried in a small cemetery at Broadstone, Dorset, England.

ON THE ATTITUDE OF MEN OF SCIENCE TOWARDS THE INVESTIGATORS OF SPIRITUALISM

(S191: 1871)

It is now generally admitted that all original investigation of Nature is useful and honorable; that the man who devotes himself to the observation of natural phenomena, of however obscure and apparently uninteresting a nature, who conducts experiments calculated to throw light upon their causes, and who fully and accurately records such observations and experiments, gains for himself a place in the roll of scientific investigators. But, strange to say, in order to merit this honorable position, he must strictly limit his inquiries within certain bounds. For should he have chanced to meet with any of those singular cases in which an individual exhibits exalted and exceptional mental capacities, appearing like the development of new senses, or those still more extraordinary phenomena which seem to prove the existence of intelligent beings, invisible and intangible to most men, yet capable, under certain conditions, of making their presence known to us; and if he devote his best energies to the study of these strange and exceptional cases, and, after long-continued inquiry and careful experiment, arrive at the conclusion that they are veritable realities, and, as such, of the highest importance to his fellow-men,--instead of being welcomed as a discoverer, or rewarded as a scientific investigator, he finds himself set down as credulous and superstitious, if not openly accused of falsehood and imposture, and his careful and oft-repeated experiments ignored, as not worth a moment's consideration.

That the public at large should thus deal with new and unpopular inquiries is not to be wondered at; but that philosophers and men of science should act in the same unscientific and unphilosophical spirit is truly extraordinary. While proclaiming loudly that the only way to acquire knowledge is by observation of facts, by experiment, and by the formation of provisional hypotheses to serve as the basis for further experiment and more extended observation, they have yet, for many years, refused to accept any facts or experiments which go to prove the existence of recondite powers in the human mind, or the action of minds not in a visible body. They have ridiculed the idea of any effects being produced by the latter cause, and have repudiated as imposture or delusion all those which appear due to the former. To show that this is really the case, I have only to quote the names of such men as Dr. Esdaile, Dr. Elliotson, Dr. Lee, Dr. Ashburner, Dr. Gregory, Dr. Reichenbach, Dr. Herbert Mayo, Dr. Haddock, Mr. H. G. Atkinson, Miss Martineau, Prof. De Morgan, William Howitt, Prof. Hare, Prof. Bush, Judge Edmonds, Robert Dale Owen, and a host of others, who, for more than twenty years, have published detailed observations and experiments, which corroborate each other in a variety of details, and agree with many facts recorded throughout history; but which observations and experiments are all ignored or denied. There has never yet been a work written in this country, which has fairly grappled with the facts addressed. It has never yet been shown, why, *à priori*, they may not be true; it has never yet been explained, how, if not true, we are to account for the vast mass of direct testimony to them. The declaration so often made or implied, that facts witnessed thousands of times by honest and intelligent men, and thousands of times carefully examined to detect fraud or delusion which has never been discovered, can not exist, because they imply a subversion of the laws of Nature, is a most weak and illogical objection, since all we know of the laws of Nature is derived from the observation of facts. No fact can possibly subvert the laws of Nature; and to declare that it does so is to declare that we have exhausted Nature, and know all her laws.

In the history of human progress, we look back in vain for a case parallel to the present one, in which the professed teachers of science have been right. The time-honored names of Galileo, Harvey, and Jenner, are associated with the record of a blind opposition to new and important truths. Franklin and Young were laughed and sneered at for discoveries which seemed wild and absurd to their scientific contemporaries. Nearer to our own day, painless operations during mesmeric trance were again and agin denounced as imposture; and the various phenomena of mesmerism, as due to collusion and fraud: yet both are now universally acknowledge to be genuine phenomena. Even such a question of pure science as the evidence of the antiquity of man has met with similar treatment till quite recently. Papers by good observers, recording facts since verified, were rejected by our scientific societies, as too absurd for publication; and careful researches now proved to be accurate were ignored, merely because they were opposed to the general belief of geologists.

It appears, then, that men of science are at least consistent in treating the phenomena of Spiritualism with contempt and derision. They have always done so with new and important discoveries; and, in every case in which the evidence has been even a tenth part of that now accumulated in favor of the phenomena of Spiritualism, they have *always been in the wrong*. It is, nevertheless, a curious psychological fact, that they do not learn by experience to detect a truth when it comes before them, or take any heed of the warnings of their greatest men against preconceived opinions as to what may, or may not, be true. Thus Humboldt declares, that "a presumptuous skepticism, which rejects facts without examination of their truth, is, in some respects, more injurious than an unquestioning incredulity." Sir Humphry Davy warns them, that "one good experiment is of more value than the ingenuity of a brain like Newton's. Facts are more useful when they contradict, than when they support, received theories." And Sir John Herschel says, that "the perfect observer in any department of Nature will have his eyes open for any occurrence, *which, according to received theories, ought not to happen*; for these are the facts which serve as clews to new discoveries." Yet in the present day, when so many things deemed absurd and impossible a few years ago have become every-day occurrences, and in direct opposition to the spirit of the advice of their most eminent teachers, a body of new and most remarkable phenomena is ignored or derided without examination, merely because, *according to received theories, such phenomena ought not to happen.*

The day will assuredly come when this will be quoted as the most striking instance on record of blind prejudice and unreasoning credulity.

ETHNOLOGY AND SPIRITUALISM

(S208: 1872)

There is only one point in Mr. Tylor's communication (*Nature*, Feb. 29,) on which it seems desirable that I should say a few words, in order that I may not be supposed to assent to what I conceive to be a most erroneous view. Mr. Tylor suggests that the phenomena that occur in the presence of what are called mediums, are or may be of the same nature as the subjective impressions of persons under the influence of a powerful mesmeriser. Five and twenty years ago I was myself a practised mesmeriser, and was able to produce on my own patients almost the whole range of phenomena which are exhibited in public as illustrative of "mesmerism" or "electro-biology." I carried on numerous experiments in private, and paid especial attention to the conditions under which the phenomena occur. During the last seven years I have had repeated opportunities of examining the phenomena that occur in the presence of so-called "mediums," often under such favourable conditions as to render trick or imposture simply impossible. I believe, therefore, I may lay claim to some qualifications for comparing the mesmeric with the mediumistic phenomena with especial reference to Mr. Tylor's suggestion, and I find that there are two great characteristics that broadly distinguish the one from the other.

1. The mesmerised patient never has *doubts* of the reality of what he sees or hears. He is like a dreamer to whom the most incongruous circumstances suggest no idea of incongruity, and he never inquires if what he thinks he perceives harmonises with his actual surroundings. He has, moreover, lost his memory of what and where he was a few moments before, and can give no account, for instance, of how he has managed to get out of a lecture-room in London to which he came as a spectator half an hour before, on to an Atlantic steamer in a hurricane, or into the recesses of a tropical forest.

The assistants at the *séances* of Mr. Home or Mrs. Guppy are not in this state, as I can personally testify, and as the almost invariable *suspicion* with which the phenomena are at first regarded clearly demonstrates. They do not lose memory of the immediately preceding events; they criticise, they examine, they take notes, they suggest tests--none of which the mesmerised patient ever does.

2. The mesmeriser has the power of acting on "certain sensitive individuals" (not on "assemblies" of people, as Mr. Tylor suggests), and all experience shows that those who are thus sensitive to any one operator are but a small proportion

of the population, and these almost always require previous manipulation with passive submission to the operator. The number who can be acted upon without such previous manipulation is very small, probably much less than one per cent. But there is no such limitation to the number of persons who simultaneously see the mediumistic phenomena. The visitors to Mr. Home or Mrs. Guppy all see whatever occurs of a physical nature, as the records of hundreds of sittings demonstrate.

The two classes of phenomena, therefore, differ fundamentally; and it is a most convincing proof of Mr. Tylor's very slender acquaintance with either of them, that he should even suggest their identity. The real connection between them is quite in an opposite direction. It is the mediums, not the assistants, who are "sensitives." They are almost always subject to the mesmeric influence, and they often exhibit all the characteristic phenomena of coma, trance, rigidity, and abnormal sense-power. Conversely, the most sensitive mesmeric patients are almost invariably mediums. The idea that it is necessary for me to inform "spiritualists" that I believe in the power of mesmerisers to make their patient believe what they please, and that this "information" might "bring about investigations leading to valuable results," is really amusing, considering that such investigations took place twenty years ago, and led to this important result--that almost all the most experienced mesmerists (Prof. Gregory,

Dr. Elliotson, Dr. Reichenbach, and many others) became spiritualists! If Mr. Tylor's suggestion had any value, these are the very men who ought to have demonstrated the subjective nature of mediumistic phenomena; but, on the contrary, as soon as they had the opportunity of personally investigating them, they all of them saw and admitted their objective reality.

OWEN'S "THE DEBATABLE LAND BETWEEN THIS WORLD AND THE NEXT"

Sixteen years ago the author of this book, then American Minister at Naples, spent the evening of the 25th of March at the house of the Russian Minister, Mons. K__, in the company of several visitors from different parts of the world, among whom were the Chevalier de F__ (the Tuscan Minister) and his lady. Madame K__ introduced the subject of automatic writing; and declared her conviction that some persons had the power of thus replying correctly to questions, the true answers to which were entirely unknown to them. It was proposed to try the experiment; and each person present accordingly took pencil and paper, and waited the result. After a few minutes one lady's hand began to move, making irregular figures on the paper. Mr. Owen proposed that questions should be asked; whereupon Madame de F__ said "Who gave me these pins?" pointing to three gold-headed pins that fastened her dress; adding "If Mrs. M__ can answer that I shall believe." After a short time the lady's pencil slowly wrote out--(the last two words being written backwards)--"The one that gives you a Maid and a

Cook. E." Madame de F__ turned pale, and cried "Magic, if there be such a thing;" and then told the company that the pins had been given her by her cousin Elizabeth, who lived at Florence, and who at her request had sent her, a few days before, a lady's maid and a cook. Mr. Owen pondered over this strange occurrence, and determined to get to the bottom of it. Mrs. M__ was not a Spiritualist. Madame de F__ had only been a few weeks in Naples, had not mentioned even her cousin's name to any one, and had the slightest possible acquaintance with Mrs. M__, having only just exchanged cards with her. She expressed the strongest conviction that the three or four facts, accurately stated in the few words written, could not possibly have become known out of her own family. Mr. Owen was then a complete sceptic; but this circumstance induced a course of study which has been continued for fifteen years, and which eventually changed the whole feelings and tenour of his life. He is now a confirmed Spiritualist; that is, he not only believes the phenomena to be real, but he has satisfied himself that they furnish a sufficient proof of a future existence for man. Yet, it may surprise some of our readers to hear, he is fully imbued with the spirit and teachings of modern science; and his book is one continued protest against the miraculous. He maintains that all these phenomena happen under law, just as much as do the various phenomena (many of them still inexplicable by science) presented by plants, animals, or man. He treats this question seriously and dispassionately, as the great question of the age; which he may well do, since he claims that it furnishes an experimental proof of immortality. He writes with the earnestness suited to such a theme, and with the sense of responsibility of one who, by long and patient study, has arrived at important truths of the highest value to his fellow men. Rationalism, he tells us, cannot object to this belief, that it contravenes the doctrine of law; for its phenomena occur strictly under law: nor yet that it assumes the existence, in spiritual matters, of that direct agency of God which the naturalist finds nowhere in the physical universe; for its revealings come to man mediately only: nor yet that it is dogmatic, exclusive, or intolerant, as Infallibility is; for its adherents adduce experimental evidence, open to all men, and gleaned after the inductive method, for the faith that is in them. He shows us how important it was for the welfare of man that the belief in such phenomena should die out when it did, and leave us free to develope the doctrine of law, and to overthrow the very idea of infallible or absolute truth in matters of religion. All the horrors of witchcraft, and all the persecutions of priests, arose from the dogma of infallibility; for if that dogma had been true, persecution would not have been a crime, but a duty. The world could not reach the fundamental truths of these phenomena, or understand their real import, as long as they believed in the devil and in their own infallibility. Now, they are able to investigate the phenomena calmly, and reason upon them logically; and it is a suggestive fact that a large proportion of investigators are persons untrammelled by dogmatic creeds, and fully imbued with the teachings of modern science and philosophy. Mr. Owen thinks that the belief in modern spiritualism is spreading as fast as can be wished, and even faster than can be expected, considering that almost every educated man is prejudiced against the very attempt to investigate it. He well remarks, that the growth of any new-born hypothesis so startling in character, resembles that of a human being. During its infancy its suggestions carry small weight. It is listened to with a smile, and set aside with little ceremony. Throughout its years of nonage it may be said to have no rights of property, no privilege of appropriation. Proofs in its favour may present themselves from time to time, but they are not deemed entitled to a judgment, by the rules of evidence; they are listened to as fresh and amusing, but they have no legal virtue; they obtain no official record; they are not placed to the credit of the minor. An adolescent hypothesis is held to be outside the limits of human justice.

One of the best features of the book, as a literary work, is the distinctness with which each piece of evidence is presented, and the fulness and logical force with which its teachings are discussed. This is so different from what is usual when ghost stories are narrated (the authors appearing afraid to contemplate the logical consequences of a story they yet maintain to be true) that it will be well to give a few of the cases in outline, with the author's summing up at length, in order to see what a well-educated and highly-intelligent man can say in favour of what is generally considered to be an exploded superstition. Let us first take an old but well-authenticated story. Lord Erskine related to Lady Morgan (herself a perfect sceptic) the following personal narrative. On arriving at Edinburgh one morning, after a considerable absence from Scotland, he met, in the street, his father's old butler, looking very pale and wan. He asked him what brought him to Edinburgh. The butler replied, "To meet your honour, and solicit your interference with my Lord, to recover a sum due to me, which the steward at the last settlement did not pay." Lord Erskine then told the butler to step with him into a bookseller's shop close by, but on turning round again he was not to be seen. Puzzled at this he found out the man's wife, who lived in Edinburgh, when he learnt for the first time that the butler was dead, and that he had told his wife on his death-bed that the steward had wronged him of some money, and that when Master Tom returned he would see her righted. This Lord Erskine promised to do, and shortly afterwards kept his promise. Lady Morgan then says, "Either Lord Erskine did or did not believe this strange story: if he did, what a strange aberration of intellect! if he did not, what a stranger aberration from truth! My opinion is that he *did* believe it." Probably hundreds of readers of this narrative by Lady Morgan have said with her, "What a strange aberration of intellect!" and have thought no more about the matter. Mr. Owen is not satisfied with this careless mode of getting over a difficulty. His remarks are as follows: "What sort of mode to deal with alleged facts is this? A gentleman distinguished in a profession of which the eminent members are the best judges of evidence in the world--a gentleman whom the hearer believes to be truthful--relates what, on a certain day, and in a certain place, both specified, he saw and heard. What he saw was the appearance of one, in life well known to him, who had been some months dead. What he heard, from the same source, was a statement in regard to matters of which previously he had known nothing whatever; which statement, on after enquiry, he learns to be strictly true; a statement, too, which had occupied and interested the mind of the deceased just before his decease. The natural inference from these facts, if they are admitted, is that, under certain circumstances which as yet we may be unable to define, those over whom the death change has passed, still interested in the concerns of earth, may, for a time at least, retain the power of occasional interference in these concerns; for example, in an effort to right an injustice done. But rather than admit such an inference--rather than accept disinterested evidence coming from a witness acknowledged to be sincere, and known to the world as eminently capable--a lady of the world assumes to explain it away by summarily referring the whole to the 'dog-ears and folds of early impression!' What human testimony cannot be set aside on the same vague and idle assumption? It is time we should learn that the hypothesis of spiritual intervention is entitled to a fair trial, and that, in conducting that trial, we have no right to disregard the ordinary rules of evidence. Either Lord Erskine, one morning in Edinburgh, issuing from a bookseller's shop, met what wore the appearance of an old family servant who had been some months dead--or else Lord Erskine lied. Either Lord Erskine heard words spoken, as if that appearance had spoken them, which words contained a certain allegation touching business which that servant, dying, had left unsettled--or else Lord Erskine lied. Either Lord Erskine ascertained, by immediate personal interrogation of the widow, that her husband, on his death-bed, had made the self-same allegation to her which the apparition made to Lord Erskine--or else Lord Erskine lied. Finally, either, as the result of this appearance and its speech, a debt found due to the person whose counterpart it was, was actually paid to his widow--or else Lord Erskine lied. But Lady Morgan expresses her conviction that Lord Erskine did not lie."

"In itself, the thing was a trifle. Thousands on thousands of such cases of petty injustice occur, and pass away unnoticed and unredressed. To the widow it was, undoubtedly, of serious moment; but I think no sensible man will imagine it a matter to justify the direct interference of God. If so, and if Lord Erskine spoke truth, *an apparition is a natural phenomenon.*"

How is such evidence as this refuted or explained away? Scores, and even hundreds, of equally well attested facts are on record, but no attempt is ever made to explain them. They are simply ignored, and, in many cases admitted to be inexplicable. Yet this is not quite satisfactory, as any reader of Mr. Owen's book will be inclined to admit. "Punch" once made a Yankee debtor say--

> "This debt I have repudiated long ago;
> 'Tis therefore settled. Yet this Britisher
> Keeps for repayment worriting me still!"

So our philosophers declare that they have long ago decided these ghost stories to be all delusion; *therefore* they need only be ignored; and they feel much "worried" that fresh evidence should be adduced and fresh converts made, some of whom are so unreasonable as to ask for a new trial on the ground that the former verdict was contrary to the evidence. Let us, however, consider another case, the parties to which are intimately known to our author, and whose character is vouched for as above suspicion.

A young lady, Miss V., while at her aunt's country mansion, was, owing to press of visitors, asked to occupy a room believed to be haunted. Miss V. accepted it willingly, being quite fearless. Awaking in the night, she saw in her room a woman in old-fashioned dress, who, after a little while, came towards her, and seemed to try in vain to speak. Miss V. became frightened, drew the clothes over her face, and when she looked again the figure had disappeared. She then jumped up, and found the door of her room locked on the inside. With the light of day the impression somewhat faded; she began to think she must have imagined or dreamt it, and in a short time thought no more of the ghost. Some time afterwards Miss V. met with a friend interested in spiritualism, and had with her several *séances*. At one of them an alleged spirit announced herself as Sarah Clarke, a name unknown to both ladies. A communication was then received to the effect that she had many years ago been housekeeper in Miss V.'s family, and had vainly endeavoured to communicate with the young lady while she was staying in the old mansion; that her object was to confess a crime of which she had been guilty, and to ask her old mistress's pardon for it. She had stolen some family plate, and begged Miss V. to tell her aunt, and beg for her forgiveness. Next time Miss V. visited her aunt, she ascertained that Sarah Clarke *had* been housekeeper in the family thirty or forty years before,--that some plate *had* mysteriously disappeared, but that Sarah was much trusted, and was never suspected. The aunt declared that if Sarah Clarke had taken it she freely forgave her. From that time the haunted chamber was free from all disturbance. Mr.

Owen comments on this, as follows: "Knowing the standing of the parties I am able to vouch for the truth of this story. Let us consider what it discloses as to the next world. There is repentance there as here. There is restless regret and sorrow for grave sin committed while here. There is anxious desire for pardon from those whom the spirit wronged during earth-life. In other words, the natural effects of evil doing follow us to our next phase of life; and, in that phase of life as in the present, we amend, and attain to better things by virtue of repentance. . . . Another corollary is, that when such spiritual phenomena present themselves, an endeavour to establish communication with the manifesting spirit may result in benefit, alike to a denizen of the other world and a disturbed inhabitant of this. In this way Mrs. Propert (see), getting rid of the midnight foot-falls, might have been in quiet possession of her villa at this day. I invite attention also to the strong proof of identity furnished by Miss V.'s story. The name of the housekeeper was unknown to both ladies when her (alleged) spirit gave the message. There was nothing to suggest such a name or such a confession as was made. Yet on enquiry both name and confession were found to correspond with facts that had taken place thirty or forty years ago; to say nothing of a new fact, tallying with all the rest--the cessation of the spiritual visits, as soon as the visitor had no longer any motive to show herself."

"How extraordinary," many readers will exclaim, "that

a man of Mr. Owen's ability should waste his time in discussing ghost stories!" It is indeed extraordinary; for do we not know all about possible and impossible spirits? Our men of science and our philosophers are not quite sure that a spirit is possible; but *if* possible, they are all quite clear that *spirits* would never behave in the ridiculously human way in which reputed ghosts invariably act. Let us, therefore, refuse to listen to these ghost stories told by people we know nothing of, and hear what Mr. Owen has to tell us of the wonders he has himself witnessed.

He spent an immense deal of time in trying to discover that gross imposture, the spirit rap, but in vain! For this purpose he once lived for a week in a medium's house, with full power to investigate. He walked all over the house with the medium, but the raps came everywhere. They sounded on the floor, walls, or ceiling of every room, on every article of furniture, on doors and windows, on the marble mantel-piece, and the steel grate. With the same medium they occurred on board a steamer, on the stool he sat on, on the keel of a small boat in the water, on the ground out of doors, on trees, and on rocks by the sea-shore. With every test that he could apply, he could find no physical cause for these sounds. Sometimes they occurred as delicate tickings, at others like blows of a sledge hammer--so tremendous that it seemed impossible any article of furniture could resist them: yet the table on which they resounded showed not a scratch!

On almost all these occasions the rooms were searched, the doors were locked, and the mediums were held fast; yet Mr. Owen could never find out the trick! How strange, when the thing is said to be so simple that our men of science will not even take the trouble to refute it!

In the matter of table-moving he had no more success. When Faraday exposed table-turning, he remarked that experimenters who thought tables even rose in the air should suspend them in a balance, and see if the weight was affected by this supposed force. Mr. Owen, at the suggestion of the late Dr. Robert Chambers, did this. Together, they suspended a table, weighing exactly 121 lbs., about 8 inches from the floor, by a powerful steelyard: two mediums were present, whose feet and hands were attended to; yet, without any contact whatever, the table, when requested, became lighter, coming down to 60 lbs., having thus lost half its weight: when requested to be made heavier it weighed 144 lbs. What are we to make of this? Two thoroughly reliable witnesses and a balance tell us one thing; but men of science say it can't be true: which are we to trust?

Continuing his researches, Mr. Owen had sittings alone with a medium. He examined the room, he locked and *sealed* the doors, and took with him privately marked slips of paper. He held the medium's hands; yet writing was somehow effected on the paper placed under the table, both in pencil and ink. Yet more; on one occasion he saw part of the writing done, by a small luminous hand on the floor, holding the pencil. On this experiment Mr. Owen remarks as follows: "Were these spiritual autographs? What else? Had I not *seen* one of them written? Had I not seen one of these slips rise higher than the table, and sink back again? Had I not felt Kate's two hands under mine at the very time when that hand wrote and that paper rose and fell? Did Kate write eight or ten lines with both her hands clasped? Did I write them with my left hand without knowing it? Or had Kate brought the slips ready written? I picked them up, and examined them critically, one by one. My private mark on one corner of each--letters of the German alphabet, written in the German character--still there! What way out? Are the senses of seeing, hearing, and touch, in sane healthy persons, unworthy to be trusted? For me, common sense bars that way out. I see nothing unlikely--not to say incredible--in the theory that God may vouchsafe to man sensible proof of his immortality. For others, to whom spiritual intercourse seems an absurdity,--for those more especially to whom the hypothesis of another life wears the aspect of a baseless dream,--let them select their own path out of the difficulty. I think that, on any path they may take, they will have to accept theories infinitely less tenable than those they decide to reject."

Mr. Owen also saw much of Mr. Foster, the medium who has names written on his hands and arms. On one occasion Mr. Foster extended his hand upon the table; it was perfectly free from any mark whatever. Gradually a faint red mark appeared on the wrist, which increased till it formed the letter F, remained visible two or three minutes, and then faded away. This was the initial letter of a name Mr. Owen had secretly written on a piece of paper, and folded up tightly, and which was mixed with about twenty others on the table. Dr. Carpenter tells us (in a letter published in "The Spiritualist" of March 15,) that this is done by first tracing the writing on the tense skin with a hard point, and then rubbing the place to bring out the red blush. But unless we are to believe that Mr. Owen and the late Dr. Robert Chambers, as well as many other careful observers who have narrated their experiences with Mr. Foster, all make grossly false or imperfect statements, this explanation by no means covers the facts; as will be admitted by all who read Mr. Owen's narrative or the evidence of Mr. E. L. Blanchard given at page 135 of the "Report of the Committee of the Dialectical Society."

Having seen so many inexplicable things himself, Mr. Owen is quite ready to believe others, when they narrate their experiences; yet he often takes an immense deal of trouble to test and confirm them, as is well shown in the marvellous story of M. Bach and the old Spinet. To be properly understood this must be read in the full detail given by Mr. Owen: in outline it is as follows: Mons. Leon

Bach purchased, at an old curiosity shop in Paris, a very ancient but beautiful *spinet*, as a present to his father, who is a great-grandson of *the* Bach, and is a composer and musical amateur. The next night the elder Bach dreamt that he saw a handsome young man, dressed in old court costume, and who told him that the spinet had been given to him by his master King Henry. He then said he would play on it an air, with words composed by the King, in memory of a lady he had greatly loved: he did so, and M. Bach woke in tears, touched by the pathos of the song. He went to sleep again; and on waking in the morning was amazed to find on his bed a sheet of paper, on which was written, in very old characters, both words and music of the song he had heard in his dream. It was said to be by Henry III., and the date inscribed on the spinet was a few years earlier. M. Bach, completely puzzled, showed the music to his friends, and among them were some spiritualists, from whom he heard, for the first time, their interpretation of the phenomena. Now comes the most wonderful part of the history. M. Bach became himself a writing medium; and through his hand was written, involuntarily, a statement that inside the spinet, in a secret niche near the key-board, was a parchment, nailed to the case, containing the lines written by King Henry when he gave the instrument to his musician. The four-line stanza, which it was said would be found on the parchment, was also given, and was followed by the signature--Baldazzarini.

Father and son then set to work to search for this hidden scroll; and after two hours' close examination found, in a narrow slit, a piece of old parchment about eleven inches by three, containing, in very old writing, nearly the same words which M. Bach had written, and signed--Henry. This parchment was taken to the Bibliothèque Impériale, and submitted to experienced antiquarians, and was pronounced to be an undoubtedly genuine autograph of Henry III.

This is the story; but Mr. Owen is not content with ascertaining these facts at first hand, and obtaining photographs of the spinet and the parchment, of both of which he gives good representations. He also sets himself to hunt up historical confirmation of the story, and after much research and many failures, he finds that Baltasarini was an Italian musician, who came to France in 1577, and was in great favour with Henry III.; that the King was passionately attached to Marie de Cleves, who became wife of the Prince de Condé; and that several of the allusions to her in the verses corresponded to what was known of her history. Other minute details were also found to be historically accurate.

Mr. Owen then carefully discusses the nature of the evidence, the character of the persons concerned, and the possibility of deception. M. Bach is an old man of high character; and to suppose that he, suddenly and without conceivable motive, planned and carried out a most elaborate and complicated imposture, is to suppose what is wholly incredible; but Mr. Owen shows further, that the circumstances are such that M. Bach could not have been an impostor, even had he been so inclined, and concludes by remarking: "I do not think dispassionate readers will accept such violent improbabilities. But if not, what interesting suggestions touching spirit-intercourse and spirit-identity connect themselves with this simple narrative of M. Bach's spinet!"

Recurring to Mr. Owen's own experiences, perhaps the most astounding is his account of the gradual formation of an apparition, distinctly visible to several spectators. Every precaution was taken to render trick or imposture impossible; yet if so, what marvel of modern science is equal to this? What natural phenomenon so worthy of investigation! Our author's remarks on this case will sufficiently indicate its nature. He says: "My faith in the reality of this appearance is not at all shaken by reflecting that a Signor Blitz, or a Robert Houdin, having a theatre at command, arranged with ready entrances and exits, with practical trap-doors, with dark lanterns in the wings, with the means of producing dissolving views, could probably reproduce all I witnessed. But here were a few ladies, in private life and in moderate circumstances, quietly meeting in two apartments which were daily used as school-rooms by one of their number, containing not even a recess where a chair could be hidden away. They meet to satisfy a laudable curiosity, admitting visitors now and then by courtesy only. No remuneration is demanded, nor, very surely, would any have been accepted. They meet, on this occasion, at my request, after having discontinued their researches for months, vexed with unjust suspicions. They allow us to lock every exit, after a close examination of the rooms. Here is neither motive nor opportunity--to say nothing of qualification--for deception. The coin of the realm may be counterfeited, but the coiners must have professional skill, an appropriate location, and expensive machinery. Nor do counterfeiters ply their unholy calling except with the prospect of large gains. Certain it is that I beheld the gradual formation of the figure; that I witnessed its movements; that I received from its hand an actual flower; that I saw the figure disappear. Add to this, that the place of its disappearance was illuminated by invisible agency, in answer to an unexpressed thought of mine."

We may particularly commend to the sceptical reader's attention the very full account of the bell-ringings at Major Moor's, at Greenwich Hospital, and other places, continuing for months, and baffling all attempts to find a cause for them; to the disturbances at Lydersterne Parsonage, continued for sixty years; and to many others, none of which have ever been explained. Mr. Owen is not content to let these matters rest (with the sceptical), or contemptuously to ignore them (with the scientific); but actually imputes them to spirits, whose agency he believes is proved by other evidence, of the nature of which we have already given some examples. This evidence, taken as a whole, proves, he thinks, that there is not habitual intercourse between the two worlds; that we seem, probably, something like apparitions to those spirits who visit us; that they often seek communion, from affection or from other motives; that they have difficulties in reaching us,-- difficulties wisely interposed, because, if spiritual intercourse were as common as earthly communion, we should many of us be dissatisfied with our lot, and neglect our earthly duties. "They seek from time to time to visit us. But coming from their world of spirits, invisible to ordinary sight, inaudible by ordinary speech, how are they to make their presence known? How are they to attract our attention? In what manner does a traveller, arriving under cloud of night before a fast-closed mansion, seek to reach the in-dwellers--seek to announce his presence? Is it not by KNOCKING or RINGING?" This is our author's reply to sneers at "rapping" and "bell-ringing" phenomena.

We have devoted so much space to a sketch of Mr. Owen's book, because, in the first place, it merits notice as a literary work of a high class; and in the second, it brings prominently before us what is either the most gigantic and mysterious of delusions or the most important of truths. In either case it deserves a full and fair discussion. Neither is such a subject out of place in a scientific journal, for, in whatever light we view it, it is really a scientific question. If a fallacy or a delusion, it is of so wide-spread a nature, and influences such numbers of well-educated and even scientific men, that we have a right to demand of science a full and satisfactory exposure of it. If a truth, then it is certainly, as Mr. Owen maintains, a science of itself; a new science, and one of the most overwhelming importance in its bearings upon philosophy, history, and religion. It is now becoming almost a common thing to acknowledge that there is a certain amount of truth in the facts; with a proviso, always, of the writer's repudiation of the spiritual theory. For my own part, the only thing that makes the facts credible on evidence *is* the spiritual theory. Mr. A., or Prof. B., or Dr. C., may state that *they know* certain of the facts are true, but that all these facts can be explained without calling in the aid of spirits. Perhaps they can. But why should I, or any other reader, accept A., B., or C.'s facts, and reject Mr. Owen's, when the former are not one whit more intrinsically probable, or supported by one iota better testimony, than the latter? Yet these latter actually *force* upon us the spiritual theory, just as the facts of Geology *force* upon us the belief in long series of ancient living forms, different from those now upon the earth. I must accept all the equally well-attested facts, of equal intrinsic probability, or reject all. I cannot believe in Cretaceous fossils as realities, and reject Silurian as freaks of nature; neither can I accept the facts B. may have witnessed, and reject those of the rest of the alphabet. Yet if all the main classes of facts are admitted, the spiritual theory appears as clearly from them as the theory of extinct animals follows from the facts presented by their fossil remains. The position of the Quarterly Reviewer is, that there are no facts worth speaking of, and, therefore, no true spiritual theory can be founded on them. This is safe ground, as long as all the evidence for the facts is carefully denied, misrepresented, or ignored. But when there are ten thousand witnesses to these facts, of whom say nine thousand are as good and competent as A. or B., it is not safe ground for A. or B. to admit just so much of the facts as they have witnessed themselves, and reject the rest. The problem we have now to solve is--how much of the facts are true. Till this is done by some better test than individual experience, it is premature to discuss what theories may or may not explain them. In the meantime, let no one prejudge the question till they have studied Mr. Owen's facts and carefully weighed his arguments.

SPIRITUALISM AND SCIENCE

(S219: 1873)

Having been named by several of your correspondents as one of the scientific men who believe in spiritualism, you will perhaps allow me to state briefly what amount of evidence has forced the belief upon me. I began the investigation about eight years ago, and I esteem it a fortunate thing that at that time the more marvellous phenomena were far less common and less accessible than they are now, because I was led to experiment largely at my own house, and among friends whom I could trust, and was able to establish to my own satisfaction, by means of a great variety of tests, the occurrence of sounds and movements not traceable to any known or conceivable physical cause. Having thus become thoroughly familiar with these undoubtedly genuine phenomena, I was able to compare them with the more powerful manifestations of several public mediums, and to recognize an identity of cause in both by means of a number of minute but highly characteristic resemblances. I was also able, by patient observation, to obtain tests of the reality of some of the more curious phenomena which appeared at the time, and still appear to me, to be conclusive. To go into details as to those experiences would require a volume, but I may, perhaps, be permitted briefly to describe one, from notes kept at the time, because it serves as an example of the complete security against deception which often occurs to the patient observer without seeking for it.

A lady who had seen nothing of the phenomena asked me and my sister to accompany her to a well-known public medium. We went, and had a sitting alone in the bright light of a summer's day. After a number of the usual raps and movements our lady friend asked if the name of the deceased person she was desirous of communicating with could be spelt out. On receiving an answer in the affirmative, the lady pointed successively to the letters of a printed alphabet while I wrote down those at which three affirmative raps occurred. Neither I nor my sister knew the name the lady wished for, nor even the names of any of her deceased relatives; her own name had not been mentioned, and she had never been near the medium before. The following is exactly what happened, except that I alter the surname, which was a very unusual one, having no authority to publish it. The letters I wrote down were of the following kind:--y n r e h n o s p m o h t. After the first three--y n r--had been taken down, my friend said, "This is nonsense, we had better begin again." Just then her pencil was at e, and raps came, when a thought struck me (having read of, but never witnessed a similar occurrence) and I said "Please go on, I think I see what is meant." When the spelling was finished I handed the paper to her, but she could see no meaning in it till I divided it at the first h, and asked her to read each portion backwards, when to her intense astonishment the name "Henry Thompson" came out, that of a deceased son of whom she had wished to hear, correct in every letter. Just about that time I had been hearing *ad nauseam* of the superhuman acuteness of mediums who detect the letters of the name the deluded visitors expect, notwithstanding all their care to pass the pencil over the letters with perfect regularity. This experience, however (for the substantial accuracy of which as above narrated I vouch), was and is, to my mind, a complete disproof of every explanation yet given of the means by which the names of deceased persons are rapped out. Of course, I do not expect any sceptic, whether scientific or unscientific, to accept such facts, of which I could give many, on my testimony, but neither must they expect me, nor the thousands of intelligent men to whom equally conclusive tests have occurred, to accept their short and easy methods of explaining them.

If I am not occupying too much of your valuable space I should like to make a few remarks on the misconceptions of many scientific men as to the nature of this inquiry, taking the letters of your correspondent Mr. Dircks as an example. In the first place, he seems to think that it is an argument against the facts being genuine that they cannot all be produced and exhibited at will; and another argument against them, that they cannot be explained by any known laws. But neither can catalepsy, the fall of meteoric stones, nor hydrophobia be produced at will; yet these are all facts, and none the less so that the first is sometimes imitated, the second was once denied, and the symptoms of the third are often greatly exaggerated, while none of them are yet brought under the domain of strict science; yet no one would make this an argument for refusing to investigate these subjects. Again, I should not have expected a scientific man to state, as a reason for not examining it, that spiritualism "is opposed to every known natural law, especially the law of gravity," and that it "sets chymistry, human physiology, and mechanics at open defiance;" when the facts simply are that the phenomena, if true, depend upon a cause or causes which can overcome or counteract the action of these several forces, just as some of these forces often counteract or overcome others; and this should surely be a strong inducement to a man of science to investigate the subject.

While not laying any claim myself to the title of "a really scientific man," there are some who deserve that epithet who have not yet been mentioned by your correspondents as at the same time spiritualists. Such I consider the late Dr. Robert Chambers, as well as Dr. Elliotson, Professor William

Gregory, of Edinburgh; and Professor Hare, of Philadelphia-
-all unfortunately deceased; while Dr. Gully, of Malvern,
as a scientific physician, and Judge Edmonds, one of the
best American lawyers, have had the most ample means of
investigation; yet all these not only were convinced of the
reality of the most marvellous facts, but also accepted the
theory of modern spiritualism as the only one which would
embrace and account for the facts. I am also acquainted with
a living physiologist of high rank as an original investigator,
who is an equally firm believer.

In conclusion I may say that, although I have heard a
great many accusations of imposture, I have never detected
it myself; and, although a large proportion of the more
extraordinary phenomena are such, that, if impostures,
they could only be performed by means of ingenious
apparatus or machinery, none has ever been discovered. I
consider it no exaggeration to say, that the main facts are
now as well established and as easily verifiable as any of the
more exceptional phenomena of nature which are not yet
reduced to law. They have a most important bearing on the
interpretation of history, which is full of narratives of similar
facts, and on the nature of life and intellect, on which physical
science throws a very feeble and uncertain light; and it is my
firm and deliberate belief that every branch of philosophy
must suffer till they are honestly and seriously investigated,
and dealt with as constituting an essential portion of the

phenomena of human nature.

A DEFENCE OF MODERN SPIRITUALISM

(S243: 1874)

It is with great diffidence, but under an imperative sense of duty, that the present writer accepts the opportunity afforded him of submitting to the readers of the Fortnightly Review some general account of a widespread movement, which, though for the most part treated with ridicule or contempt, he believes to embody truths of the most vital importance to human progress. The subject to be treated is of such vast extent, the evidence concerning it is so varied and so extraordinary, the prejudices that surround it are so inveterate, that it is not possible to do it justice without entering into considerable detail. The reader who ventures on the perusal of the succeeding pages may, therefore, have his patience tried; but if he is able to throw aside his preconceived ideas of what is possible and what is impossible, and in the acceptance or rejection of the evidence submitted to him will carefully weigh and be solely guided by the nature of the concurrent testimony, the writer ventures to believe that he will not find his time and patience ill-bestowed.

Few men, in this busy age, have leisure to read massive volumes devoted to special subjects. They gain much of their general knowledge, outside the limits of their profession or of any peculiar study, by means of periodical literature; and, as a rule, they are supplied with copious and accurate, though general, information. Some of our best thinkers and workers make known the results of their researches to the readers of magazines and reviews; and it is seldom that a writer whose information is meagre, or obtained at second-hand, is permitted to come before the public in their pages as an authoritative teacher. But as regards the subject we are now about to consider, this rule has not hitherto been followed. Those who have devoted many years to an examination of its phenomena have been, in most cases, refused a hearing; while men who have bestowed on it no adequate attention, and are almost wholly ignorant of the researches of others, have alone supplied the information to which a large proportion of the public have had access. In support of this statement it is necessary to refer, with brief comments, to some of the more prominent articles in which the phenomena and pretensions of Spiritualism have been recently discussed.

At the beginning of the present year the readers of this Review were treated to "Experiences of Spiritualism," by a writer of no mean ability, and of thoroughly advanced views.

He assures his readers that he "conscientiously endeavoured to qualify himself for speaking on this subject" by attending five séances, the details of several of which he narrates; and he comes to the conclusion that mediums are by no means ingenious deceivers, but "jugglers of the most vulgar order;" that the "spiritualistic mind falls a victim to the most patent frauds," and greedily "accepts jugglery as manifestations of spirits"; and, lastly, that the mediums are as credulous as their dupes, and fall straightway into any trap that is laid for them. Now, on the evidence before him, and on the assumption that no more or better evidence would have been forthcoming had he devoted fifty instead of five evenings to the inquiry, the conclusions of Lord Amberley are perfectly logical; but, so far from what he witnessed being a "specimen of the kind of manifestations by which spiritualists are convinced," a very little acquaintance with the literature of the subject would have shown him that no spiritualist of any mark was ever convinced by any quantity of such evidence. In an article published since Lord Amberley's--in *London Society* for February--the author, a barrister and well-known literary man, says:--

"It was difficult for me to give in to the idea that solid objects could be conveyed, invisibly, through closed doors, or that heavy furniture could be moved without the interposition of hands. Philosophers will say these things are absolutely impossible; nevertheless, it is absolutely certain that they do occur. I have met in the houses of private friends, as witnesses of these phenomena, persons whose testimony would go for a good deal in a court of justice. They have included peers, members of parliament, diplomatists of the highest rank, judges, barristers, physicians, clergymen, members of learned societies, chemists, engineers, journalists, and thinkers of all sorts and degrees. They have suggested and carried into effect tests of the most rigid and satisfactory character. The media (all non-professional) have been searched before and after séances. The precaution has even been taken of providing them unexpectedly with other apparel. They have been tied; they have been sealed; they have been secured in every cunning and dexterous manner that ingenuity could devise, but no deception has been discovered and no imposture brought to light. Neither was there any motive for imposture. No fee or reward of any kind depended upon the success or non-success of the manifestations."

Now here we have a nice question of probabilities. We must either believe that Lord Amberley is almost infinitely more acute than Mr. Dunphy and his host of eminent friends--so that after five séances (most of them failures) he has got to the bottom of a mystery in which they, notwithstanding their utmost endeavours, still hopelessly flounder--or, that the noble lord's acuteness does not surpass the combined acuteness of all these persons; in which case their much larger experience, and their having witnessed many things

Lord Amberley has not witnessed, must be held to have the greater weight, and to show, at all events, that all mediums are not "jugglers of the most vulgar order."

In October last the *New Quarterly Magazine*, in its opening number, had an article entitled "A Spiritualistic Séance;" but which proved to be an account of certain ingenious contrivances by which some of the phenomena usual at séances were imitated, and both spiritualists and sceptics deceived and confounded. This appears at first sight to be an exposure of Spiritualism, but it is really very favourable to its pretensions; for it goes on the assumption that the marvellous phenomena witnessed do really occur, but are produced by various mechanical contrivances. In this case the rooms above, below, and at the side of that in which the séance was held had to be prepared with specially constructed machinery, with assistants to work it. The apparatus, as described, would cost at least £100, and would then only serve to produce a few fixed phenomena, such as happen frequently in private houses and at the lodgings of mediums who have not exclusive possession of any of the adjoining rooms, or the means of obtaining expensive machinery and hired assistants. The article bears internal evidence of being altogether a fictitious narrative; but it helps to demonstrate, if any demonstration is required, that the phenomena which occur under such protean forms and varied conditions, and in private houses quite as often as at the apartments of the mediums, are in no way produced by machinery.

Perhaps the most prominent recent attack on Spiritualism was that in the *Quarterly Review* for October, 1871, which is known to have been written by an eminent physiologist, and did much to blind the public to the real nature of the movement. This article, after giving a light sketch of the reported phenomena, entered into some details as to planchette-writing and table-lifting--facts on which no spiritualist depends as evidence to a third party--and then proceeded to define its standpoint as follows:--

"Our position, then, is that the so-called spiritual communications come from *within*, not from without, the individuals who suppose themselves to be the recipients of them; that they belong to the class termed 'subjective' by physiologists and psychologists, and that the movements by which they are expressed, whether the tilting of tables or the writing of planchettes, are really produced by their own muscular action exerted independently of their own wills and quite unconsciously to themselves."

Several pages are then devoted to accounts of séances which, like Lord Amberley's, were mostly failures; and to the experiences of a Bath clergyman who believed that the communications came from devils; and, generally, such weak and inconclusive phenomena only are adduced as can be easily explained by the well-worn formulæ of "unconscious cerebration," "expectant attention," and "unconscious muscular action." A few of the more startling physical phenomena are mentioned merely to be discredited and the judgment of the witnesses impugned; but no attempt is made to place before the reader any information as to the amount or the weight of the testimony to such phenomena, or to the long series of diverse phenomena which lead up to and confirm them. Some of the experiments of Professor Hare and Mr. Crookes are quoted, and criticised in the spirit of assuming that these experienced physicists were ignorant of the simplest principles of mechanics, and failed to use the most ordinary precautions. Of the numerous and varied cases on record of heavy bodies being moved without direct or indirect contact by any human being, no notice is taken, except so far as quoting Mr. C. F. Varley's statement, that he had seen, in broad daylight, a small table moved ten feet, with no one near it but himself, and not touched by him--"as an example of the manner in which minds of this limited order are apt to become the dupes of their own imaginings."

This article, like the others here referred to, shows in the writer an utter forgetfulness of the maxim, that an argument is not answered till it is answered at its best. Amid the vast mass of recorded facts now accumulated by spiritualists there is, of course, much that is weak and inconclusive, much that is of no value as evidence, except to those who have independent reasons for faith in them. From this undigested mass it is the easiest thing in the world to pick out arguments that can be refuted, and facts that can be explained away; but what is that to the purpose? It is not these that have convinced any one; but those weightier, oft-repeated and oft-tested facts which the writers referred to invariably ignore.

Professor Tyndall has also given the world (in his "Fragments of Science," published in 1871) some account of his attempt to investigate these phenomena. Again we have a minute record of a séance which was a failure; and in which the Professor, like Lord Amberley, easily imposed on some too credulous spiritualists by improvising a few manifestations of his own. The article in question is dated as far back as 1864. We may therefore conclude that the Professor has not seen much of the subject; nor can he have made himself acquainted with what others have seen and carefully verified, or he would hardly have thought his communication worthy of the place it occupies among original researches and positive additions to human knowledge. Both its facts and its reasonings have been well replied to by Mr. Patrick Fraser Alexander, in his little work entitled, "Spiritualism; a Narrative and a Discussion," which we recommend to those who care to see how a very acute yet unprejudiced mind looks at the phenomena, and how inconclusive, even from a scientific standpoint, are the experiences adduced by Professor Tyndall.

The discussion in the *Pall Mall Gazette* in 1868, and a

considerable private correspondence, indicates that scientific men almost invariably assume, that in this inquiry they should be permitted, at the very outset, to impose conditions; and if, under such conditions, nothing happens, they consider it a proof of imposture or delusion. But they well know that, in all other branches of research, nature, not they, determines the essential conditions without a compliance with which no experiment will succeed. These conditions have to be learnt by a patient questioning of nature, and they are different for each branch of science. How much more may they be expected to differ in an inquiry which deals with subtle forces of the nature of which the physicist is wholly and absolutely ignorant! To ask to be allowed to deal with these unknown phenomena as he has hitherto dealt with known phenomena, is practically to prejudge the question, since it assumes that both are governed by the same laws.

From the sketch which has now been given of the recent treatment of the subject by popular and scientific writers, we can summarise pretty accurately their mental attitude in regard to it. They have seen very little of the phenomena themselves, and they cannot believe that others have seen much more. They have encountered people who are easily deceived by a little unexpected trickery, and they conclude that the convictions of spiritualists generally are founded on phenomena produced, either consciously or unconsciously, in a similar way. They are so firmly convinced on *à priori* grounds that the more remarkable phenomena said to happen do not really happen, that they will back their conviction against the direct testimony of any body of men; preferring to believe that they are all the victims of some mysterious delusion whenever imposture is out of the question. To influence persons in this frame of mind, it is evident that *more* personal testimony to isolated facts is utterly useless. They have, to use the admirable expression of Dr. Carpenter, "no place in the existing fabric of their thought into which such facts can be fitted." It is necessary therefore to modify the "fabric of thought" itself; and it appears to the present writer that this can best be done by a general historic sketch of the subject; and by showing, by separate lines of inquiry, how wide and varied is the evidence, and how remarkably these lines converge towards one uniform conclusion. The endeavour will be made to indicate, by typical examples of each class of evidence and without unnecessary detail, the cumulative force of the argument.

Historical Sketch.

Modern Spiritualism dates from March, 1848; it being then that, for the first time, intelligent communications were held with the unknown cause of the mysterious knockings and other sounds, similar to those which had disturbed the Mompesson and Wesley families in the seventeenth and eighteenth centuries. This discovery was made by Miss Kate

Fox, a girl of nine years old, and the first recognised example of an extensive class now known as mediums. It is worthy of remark, that this very first "modern spiritual manifestation" was subjected to the test of unlimited examination by all the inhabitants of the village of Hydesville, New York. Though all were utter sceptics, no one could discover any cause for the noises, which continued, though with less violence, when all the children had left the house. Nothing is more common than the remark, that it is absurd and illogical to impute noises, of which we cannot discover the cause, to the agency of spirits. So it undoubtedly is when the noises are merely noises; but is it so illogical when these noises turn out to be signals, and signals which spell out a fact, which fact, though wholly unknown to all present, turns out to be true? Yet, on this very first occasion, twenty-six years ago, the signals declared that a murdered man was buried in the cellar of the house; it indicated the exact spot in the cellar under which the body lay; and upon digging there, at a depth of six or seven feet, considerable portions of a human skeleton were found. Yet more; the name of the murdered man was given, and it was ascertained that such a person had visited that very house and had disappeared five years before, and had never been heard of since. The signals further declared that he, the murdered man, was the signaller; and as all the witnesses had satisfied themselves that the signals were not made by any living person or by any assignable cause, the logical conclusion from the facts was, that it *was* the spirit[2] of the murdered man; although such a conclusion might be to some in the highest degree improbable, and to others in the highest degree absurd.

The Misses Fox now became involuntary mediums, and the family (which had removed to the city of Rochester) were accused of imposture, and offered to submit the children to examination by a committee of townsmen appointed in public meeting. Three committees were successively appointed; the last, composed of violent sceptics who had accused the previous committees of stupidity or connivance. But all three, after unlimited investigation, were forced to declare that the cause of the phenomena was undiscoverable. The sounds occurred on the wall and floor while the mediums, after being thoroughly searched by ladies, "stood on pillows, barefooted, and with their clothes tied round their ankles." The last and most sceptical committee reported that, "They had heard sounds, and failed utterly to discover their origin. They had proved that neither machinery nor imposture had been used; and their questions, *many of them being mental,* were answered correctly." When we consider that the mediums were two children under twelve years of age, and the examiners utterly sceptical American citizens, thoroughly resolved to detect imposture, and urged on by excited public meetings, it may perhaps be considered that even at this early stage the question of imposture or delusion was pretty well settled in the negative.

In a short time persons who sat with the Misses Fox found themselves to have similar powers in a greater or less degree; and in two or three years the movement had spread over a large part of the United States, developing into a variety of strange forms, encountering the most violent scepticism and the most rancorous hostility, yet always progressing, and making converts even among the most enlightened and best educated classes. In 1851, some of the most intelligent men in New York--judges, senators, doctors, lawyers, merchants, clergymen, and authors--formed themselves into a society for investigation. Judge Edmunds was one of these; and a sketch of the kind and amount of evidence that was required to convince him will be given further on. In 1854 a second spiritual society was formed in New York. It had the names of four judges and two physicians among its vice-presidents, showing that the movement had by this time become respectable, and that men in high social positions were not afraid of identifying themselves with it. A little later Professor Mapes, an eminent agricultural chemist, was led to undertake the investigation of Spiritualism. He formed a circle of twelve friends, most of them men of talent and sceptics, who bound themselves to sit together weekly, with a medium, twenty times. For the first eighteen evenings the phenomena were so trivial and unsatisfactory, that most of the party felt disgusted at the loss of time; but the last two sittings produced phenomena of so startling a character, that the investigation was continued by the same circle *for four years, and all became spiritualists.*

By this time the movement had spread into every part of the Union, and, notwithstanding that its adherents were abused as impostors or dupes, that they were in several cases expelled from colleges and churches, and were confined as lunatics, and that the whole thing was "explained" over and over again, it has continued to spread up to the present hour. The secret of this appears to have been, that the explanations given never applied to the phenomena continually occurring, and of which there were numerous witnesses. A medium was raised in the air in a crowded room in full daylight. ("Modern American Spiritualism," .) A scientific sceptic prepared a small portable apparatus by which he could produce an instantaneous illumination; and, taking it to a dark séance at which numerous musical instruments were played, suddenly lighted up the room while a large drum was being violently beaten, in the certain expectation of revealing the impostor to the whole company. But what they all saw was the drumstick itself beating the drum, with no human being near it. It struck a few more blows, then rose into the air and descended gently on to the shoulder of a lady. (Same work, .) At Toronto, Canada, in a well-lighted room, an accompaniment to a song was played on a closed and locked piano. (Same work, .) Communications were given in raised letters on the arm of an ignorant servant girl who often could not read them. They sometimes appeared while she was at her household work, and after being read by her master or mistress would disappear. (Same work, .) Letters closed in any number of envelopes, sealed up or even pasted together over the whole of the written surface, were read and answered by certain mediums in whom this special power was developed. It mattered not what language the letters were written in; and it is upon record that letters in German, Greek, Hebrew, Arabic, Chinese, French, Welsh, and Mexican, have been correctly answered in the corresponding languages by a medium who knew none of them. (Judge Edmunds's "Letters on Spiritualism," p -103, Appendix.) Other mediums drew portraits of deceased persons whom they had never known or heard of. Others healed diseases. But those who helped most to spread the belief were, perhaps, the trance speakers, who, in eloquent and powerful language, developed the principles and the uses of Spiritualism, answered objections, spread abroad a knowledge of the phenomena, and thus induced sceptics to inquire into the facts; and inquiry was almost invariably followed by conversion. Having repeatedly listened to three of these speakers who have visited this country, I can bear witness that they fully equal, and not unfrequently surpass, our best orators and preachers; whether in finished eloquence, in close and logical argument, or in the readiness with which appropriate and convincing replies are made to all objectors. They are also remarkable for the perfect courtesy and suavity of their manner, and for the extreme patience and gentleness with which they meet the most violent opposition and the most unjust accusations.

Men of the highest rank and greatest ability became convinced by these varied phenomena. No amount of education, of legal, medical, or scientific training, was proof against the overwhelming force of the facts, whenever these facts were systematically and perseveringly inquired into. The number of spiritualists in the Union is, according to those who have the best means of judging, from eight to eleven millions. This is the estimate of Judge Edmonds, who has had extensive correspondence on the subject with every part of the United States. The Hon. R. D. Owen, who has also had great opportunities of knowing the facts, considers it to be approximately correct; and it is affirmed by the editors of the "Year Book of Spiritualism" for 1871. These numbers have been held to be absurdly exaggerated by persons having less information, especially by strangers who have made superficial inquiries in America; but it must be remembered that the spiritualists are to a very limited extent an organized body, and that the mass of them make no public profession of their belief, but still remain members of some denominational church--circumstances that would greatly deceive an outsider. Nevertheless, the organization is of considerable extent. There were in America, in 1870, 20 State associations and 105 societies of spiritualists, 207 lecturers, and about the same number of public mediums.

In other parts of the world the movement has progressed more or less rapidly. Several of the more celebrated American mediums have visited this country, and not only made converts in all classes of society, but led to the formation of private circles and the discovery of mediumistic power in hundreds of families. There is scarcely a city or a considerable town in continental Europe at the present moment where spiritualists are not reckoned by hundreds, if not by thousands. There are said, on good authority, to be fifty thousand avowed spiritualists in Paris and ten thousand in Lyons; and the numbers in this country may be roughly estimated by the fact that there are four exclusively spiritual periodicals, one of which has a circulation of five thousand weekly.

Deductions from the Preceding Sketch.

Before proceeding to a statement of the evidence which has convinced the more educated and more sceptical converts, let us consider briefly the bearing of the undoubted fact, that (to keep within bounds) many thousands of well-informed men, belonging to all classes of society and all professions, have, in each of the great civilised nations of the world, acknowledged the objective reality of these phenomena;

although, almost without exception, they at first viewed them with dislike or contempt, as impostures or delusions. There is nothing parallel to it in the history of human thought; because there never before existed so strong and apparently so well-founded a conviction that phenomena of this kind never have happened and never can happen. It is often said, that the number of adherents to a belief is no proof of its truth. This remark justly applies to most religions whose arguments appeal to the emotions and the intellect but not to the evidence of the senses. It is equally just as applied to a great part of modern science. The almost universal belief in gravitation, and in the undulatory theory of light, does not render them in any degree more probable; because very few indeed of the believers have tested the facts which most convincingly demonstrate those theories, or are able to follow out the reasoning by which they are demonstrated. It is for the most part a blind belief accepted upon authority. But with these spiritual phenomena the case is very different. They are to most men so new, so strange, so incredible, so opposed to their whole habit of thought, so apparently opposed to the pervading scientific spirit of the age, that they cannot and do not accept them on second-hand evidence, as they do almost every other kind of knowledge. The thousands or millions of spiritualists, therefore, represent to a very large extent men who have witnessed, examined, and tested the evidence for themselves, over and over and over again, till that which they had at first been unable to admit *could* be true, they have at last been compelled to acknowledge *is* true. This accounts for the utter failure of all the attempted "exposures" and "explanations" to convince one solitary believer of his error. The exposers and explainers have never got beyond those first difficulties which constitute the *pons asinorum* of Spiritualism, which every believer has to get over, but at which early stage of investigation no converts are ever made. By explaining table-turning, or table-tilting, or raps, you do not influence a man who was never convinced by these, but who, in broad daylight, sees objects move without contact, and behave as if guided by intelligent beings; and who sees this in a variety of forms, in a variety of places, and under such varied and stringent conditions, as to make the fact to him just as real as the movement of iron to the magnet. By explaining automatic writing (which itself convinces no one but the writer, and not always even him), you do not affect the belief of the man who has obtained writing when neither pencil nor paper were touched by any one; or has seen a hand not attached to any human body take up a pencil and write; or, as Mr. Andrew Leighton, of Liverpool, testifies, has seen a pencil rise of itself on a table and write the words--"*And is this world of strife to end in dust at last?*" Thus it is that there are so few recantations or perverts in Spiritualism; so few, that it may be truly said there are none. After much inquiry and reading I can find no example of a man who, having acquired a good personal knowledge of all the chief phases of the phenomena, has subsequently come to disbelieve in their reality. If the "explanations" and "exposures" were good for anything, or if it were an imposture to expose or a delusion to explain, this could not be the case, because there are numbers of men who have become convinced of the facts, but who have not accepted the spiritual theory. These are, for the most part, in an uncomfortable and unsettled frame of mind, and would gladly welcome an explanation which really explained anything--but they find it not. As an eminent example of this class, I may mention Dr. J. Lockhart Robertson, long one of the editors of the *Journal of Mental Science*--a physician who, having made mental disease his special study, would not be easily taken in by any psychological delusions. The phenomena he witnessed fourteen years ago were of a violent character; a very strong table being, at his own request and in his own house, broken to pieces while he held the medium's hands. He afterwards himself tried to break a remaining leg of the table, but failed to do so after exerting all his strength. Another table was tilted over while all the party sat on it. He subsequently had a sitting with Mr. Home, and witnessed the usual phenomena occurring with that extraordinary medium--such as the accordion playing "most wonderful music without any human agency," "a shadow hand, not that of any one present, which lifts a pencil and writes with it," &c., &c.; and he says that he can "no more doubt the physical manifestations of (so called) Spiritualism than he would any other fact--as, for example, the fall of an apple to the ground of which his senses informed him." His record of these phenomena, with the confirmation by a friend who was present, is published in the "Dialectical Society's Report on Spiritualism," ; and, at a meeting of Spiritualists in 1870, he reasserted the facts, but denied their spiritual origin. To such a man the Quarterly Reviewer's explanations are worthless; yet it may be safely said, that every advanced Spiritualist has seen more remarkable, more varied, and even more inexplicable phenomena than those recorded by Dr. Robertson, and are therefore still further out of reach of the arguments referred to, which are indeed only calculated to convince those who know little or nothing of the matter.

Evidence of the Facts.

The subject of the evidences of the objective phenomena of Spiritualism is such a large one that it will be only possible here to give a few typical examples, calculated to show how wide is their range, and how conclusively they reach every objection that the most sceptical have brought against them. This may perhaps be best done by giving, in the first place, an outline of the career of two or three well-known mediums; and, in the second, a sketch of the experiences and investigations of a few of the more remarkable converts to Spiritualism.

Career of Remarkable Mediums.--Miss Kate Fox, the little girl of nine years old, who, as already stated, was the first "medium" in the modern sense of the term, has continued to possess the same power for twenty-six years. At the very earliest stages of the movement, sceptic after sceptic, committee after committee, endeavoured to discover "the trick;" but if it was a trick this little girl baffled them all, and the proverbial acuteness of the Yankee was of no avail. In 1860, when Dr. Robert Chambers visited America, he suggested to his friend, Robert Dale Owen, the use of a balance to test the lifting power. They accordingly, without pre-arrangement with the medium, took with them a powerful steelyard, and suspended from it a dining-table weighing 121 pounds. Then, under a bright gas-light, the feet of the two mediums (Miss Fox and her sister) being both touched by the feet of the gentlemen, and the hands of all present being held over but not touching the table, it was made lighter or heavier at request, so as to weigh at one time only 60, at another 134 pounds. This experiment, be it remembered, was identical with one proposed by Faraday himself as being conclusive. Mr. Owen had many sittings with Miss Fox for the purpose of test; and the precautions he took were extraordinary. He sat with her alone; he frequently changed the room without notice; he examined every article of furniture; he locked the doors and fastened them with strips of paper privately sealed; he held both the hands of the medium. Under these conditions various phenomena occurred, the most remarkable being the illumination of a piece of paper (which he had brought himself, cut of a peculiar size, and privately marked), showing a dark hand writing on the floor. The paper afterwards rose up on to the table with legible writing upon it, containing a promise which was subsequently verified. ("Debateable Land," .)

But Miss Fox's powers were most remarkably shown in the séances with Mr. Livermore, a well-known New York banker, and an entire sceptic before commencing these experiments. These sittings were more than three hundred in number, extending over five years. They took place in four different houses (Mr. Livermore's and the medium's being both changed during this period), under tests of the most rigid description. The chief phenomenon was the appearance of a tangible, visible, and audible figure of Mr. Livermore's deceased wife, sometimes accompanied by a male figure, purporting to be Dr. Franklin. The former figure was often most distinct and absolutely life-like. It moved various objects in the room. It wrote messages on cards. It was sometimes formed out of a luminous cloud, and again vanished before the eyes of the witnesses. It allowed a portion of its dress to be cut off, which though at first of strong and apparently material gauzy texture, yet in a short time melted away and became invisible. Flowers which melted away were also given. These phenomena occurred best when Mr. L. and the medium were alone; but two witnesses were occasionally admitted, who tested everything and confirmed Mr. L.'s testimony. One of these was Mr. Livermore's physician, the other his brother-in-law; the latter previously a sceptic. The details of these wonderful séances were published in the *Spiritual Magazine* in 1862 and 1863; and the more remarkable are given in Owen's "Debateable Land," from which work a good idea may be formed of the great variety of the phenomena that occurred and the stringent character of the tests employed.

Miss Fox recently came to England, and here also her powers have been tested by a competent man of science, and found to be all that has been stated. She is now married to an English barrister, and some of the strange phenomena which have so long accompanied her, attach themselves to her infant child, even when its mother is away, to the great alarm of the nurse. We have here, therefore, a career of twenty-six years of mediumship of the most varied and remarkable character; mediumship which has been scrutinized and tested from the first hour of its manifestation down to this day, and with one invariable result--that no imposture or attempt at imposture has ever been discovered, and no cause ever been suggested that will account for the phenomena except that advanced by Spiritualists.

Mr. Daniel D. Home is perhaps the best known

medium in the world; and his powers have been open to examination for at least twenty years. Nineteen years ago Sir David Brewster and Lord Brougham had a sitting with him--sufficiently acute and eminent observers, and both, of course, thorough sceptics. In the "Home Life of Sir David Brewster," we have, fortunately, his own record of this sitting made *at the time*, although six months later, in a letter to the *Morning Advertiser*, he made the contradictory statement, "I saw enough to satisfy myself they could all be produced by human hands and feet." He says: "The table actually rose from the ground when no hand was upon it;" and "a small hand-bell was laid down with its mouth on the carpet, and it actually rang when nothing could have touched it. The bell was then placed on the other side, still upon the carpet, and it came over to me and placed itself in my hand. It did the same to Lord Brougham." And he adds, speaking for both, "We could give no explanation of them, and could not conjecture how they could be produced by any kind of mechanism." Coming from the author of "Letters on Natural Magic," this is pretty good testimony.

These and far more marvellous phenomena have been repeated from that day to this, many thousands of times, and almost always in private houses at which Mr. Home visits. Everybody testifies to the fact that he offers the most ample facilities for investigation; and to this I can myself bear witness, having been invited by him to examine as closely as I pleased an accordion, held by his one hand, keys downward, and in that position playing very sweetly. But, perhaps, the best attested and most extraordinary phenomenon connected with Mr. Home's mediumship is what is called the fire test. In a state of trance he takes a glowing coal from the hottest part of a bright fire, and carries it round the room, so that every one may see and feel that it is a real one. This is testified by Mr. H. D. Jencken, Lord Lindsay, Lord Adare, Miss Douglas, Mr. S. C. Hall, and many others. But, more strange still, when in this state he can detect the same power in other persons, or convey it to them. A lump of red-hot coal was once placed on Mr. S. C. Hall's head in the presence of Lord Lindsay and four other persons. Mrs. Hall, in a communication to the Earl of Dunraven (given in the *Spiritual Magazine*, 1870,), says:--

"Mr. Hall was seated nearly opposite to where I sat; and I saw Mr. Home, after standing about half a minute at the back of Mr. Hall's chair, deliberately place the lump of burning coal on his head! I have often wondered that I was not frightened, but I was not; I had perfect faith that he would not be injured. Some one said, 'Is it not hot?' Mr. Hall answered, 'Warm, but not hot.' Mr. Home had moved a little way, but returned, still in a trance; he smiled, and seemed quite pleased, and then proceeded to draw up Mr. Hall's white hair over the red coal. The white hair had the appearance of silver thread over the red coal. Mr. Home drew the hair into a sort of pyramid, the coal, still red, showing beneath the hair."

When taken off the head, which it had not in the slightest degree injured or singed the hair, others attempted to touch it and were burnt. Lord Lindsay and Miss Douglas have also had hot coals placed in their hands, and they describe them as feeling rather cold than hot; though at the same time they burn any one else, and even scorch the face of the holder if approached too closely. The same witnesses also testify that Mr. Home has placed red-hot coals inside his waistcoat without scorching his clothes, and has put his face into the middle of the fire, his hair falling into the flames, yet not being the least singed. The same power of resisting fire can be temporarily given to inanimate objects. Mr. H. Nisbet of Glasgow states (*Human Nature*, Feb., 1870), that in his own house, in January, 1870, Mr. Home placed a red-hot coal in the hands of a lady and gentleman, which they only felt warm; and then placed the same piece on a folded newspaper, burning a hole through eight layers of paper. He then took a fresh and blazing coal and laid it on the same newspaper, carrying it about the room for three minutes, when the paper was found, this time, not to have been the least burnt. Lord Lindsay further declares--and as one of the few noblemen who do real scientific work his evidence must be of some value--that on eight occasions he has had red-hot coals placed on his own hand by Home without injury. Mr.

W. H. Harrison (*Spiritualist*, March 15th, 1870), saw him take a large coal, which covered the palm of his hand, and stood six or seven inches high. As he walked about the room it threw a ruddy glow on the walls, and when he came to the table with it, the heat was felt in the faces of all present. The coal was thus held for five minutes. These phenomena have now happened scores of times in the presence of scores of witnesses. They are facts of the reality of which there can be no doubt; and they are altogether inexplicable by the known laws of physiology and heat.

The powers of Mr. Home have lately been independently tested by Serjeant Cox and Mr. Crookes, and both these gentlemen emphatically proclaim that he invites tests and courts examination. Serjeant Cox, in his own house, has had a new accordion (purchased by himself that very day) play by itself, in his own hand, while Mr. Home was playing the piano. Mr. Home then took the accordion in his left hand, holding it with the keys downwards while playing the piano with his right hand, "and it played beautifully in accompaniment to the piano, for at least a quarter of an hour." ("What Am I?" vol. ii. .)

As to the possibility of these things being produced by trick, if further evidence than their mere statement be required, we have the following by Mr. T. Adolphus Trollope, who says, "I may also mention that Bosco, one of the greatest professors of legerdemain ever known, in a conversation with me upon the subject, utterly scouted the idea of the possibility of such phenomena as I saw produced by Mr. Home being performed by any of the resources of his art."

Mr. Home's life has been to a great extent a public one. He has spent much of his time as a guest in the houses of people of rank and talent. He numbers among his friends many who are eminent in science, art, and literature--men certainly not inferior in perceptive or reasoning power to those who, not having witnessed the phenomena, disbelieve in their occurrence. For twenty years he has been exposed to the keen scrutiny and never-ceasing suspicion of innumerable inquirers; yet no proof has ever been given of trickery, no particle of machinery or apparatus ever been detected. But the phenomena are so stupendous that, if impostures, they could only be performed by machinery of the most elaborate, varied, and cumbrous nature, requiring the aid of several assistants and confederates. The theory that they are delusions is equally untenable, unless it is admitted that there is no possible means of distinguishing delusion from reality.

The last medium to whose career I shall call attention is Mrs. Guppy (formerly Miss Nichol), and in this case I can give some personal testimony. I knew Miss Nichol before she had ever heard of spiritualism, table-rapping, or anything of the kind, and we first discovered her powers on asking her to sit for experiment in my house. This was in November, 1866, and for some months we had constant sittings, and I was able to watch and test the progress of her development. I first satisfied myself of the rising of a small table completely off the floor, when three or four persons (including Miss N.) placed their hands on it. I tested this by secretly attaching threads or thin strips of paper underneath the claws, so that they must be broken if any one attempted to raise the table with their feet--the only available means of doing so. The table still rose a full foot off the floor in broad daylight. In order to show this to friends with less trouble, I made a cylinder of hoops and brown paper, in which I placed the table so as to keep feet and dresses away from it while it rose, which it did as freely as before. Perhaps more marvellous was the placing of Miss N. herself on the table; for although this always happened in the dark, yet, under the conditions to be named, deception was impossible. I will relate one sitting of which I have notes. We sat in a friend's house, round a centre table, under a glass chandelier. A friend of mine, but a perfect stranger to all the rest, sat next Miss Nichol and held both her hands. Another person had matches ready to strike a light when required. What occurred was as follows:--First, Miss Nichol's chair was drawn away from under her, and she was obliged to stand up, my friend still holding both her hands. In a minute or two more I heard a slight sound, such as might be produced by a person placing a wine-glass on the table, and at the same time a very slight rustling of clothes and tinkling of the glass pendants of the chandelier. Immediately my friend said, "She is gone from me." A light was at once struck, and we found Miss N. quietly seated in her chair on the centre of the table, her head just touching the chandelier. My friend declared that Miss N. seemed to glide noiselessly out of his hands. She was very stout and heavy, and to get her chair on the table, to get upon it herself, in the dark, noiselessly, and almost instantaneously, with five or six persons close around her, appeared, and still appears to me, knowing her intimately, to be physically impossible.

Another very curious and beautiful phenomenon was the production of delicate musical sounds, without any object calculated to produce them being in the room. On one occasion a German lady, who was a perfect stranger to Miss Nichol, and had never been at a séance before, was present. She sang several German songs, and most delicate music, like a fairy musical-box, accompanied her throughout. She sang four or five different songs of her own choice, and all were so accompanied. This was in the dark, but hands were joined all the time.

The most remarkable feature of this lady's mediumship is the production of flowers and fruits in closed rooms. The first time this occurred was at my own house, at a very early stage of her development. All present were my own friends. Miss Nichol had come early to tea, it being mid-winter, and she had been with us in a very warm gas-lighted room four hours before the flowers appeared. The essential fact is, that upon a bare table in a small room closed and dark (the adjoining room and passage being well lighted), a quantity of flowers appeared, which were not there when we put out the gas a few minutes before. They consisted of anemones, tulips, chrysanthemums, Chinese primroses, and several ferns. All were absolutely fresh, as if just gathered from a conservatory. They were covered with a fine cold dew. Not a petal was crumpled or broken, not the most delicate point or pinnule of the ferns was out of place. I dried and preserved the whole, and have, attached to them, the attestation of all present that they had no share, as far as they knew, in bringing the flowers into the room. I believed at the time, and still believe, that it was absolutely impossible for Miss N. to have concealed them so long, to have kept them so perfect, and, above all, to produce them covered throughout with a most beautiful coating of dew, just like that which collects on the outside of a tumbler when filled with very cold water on a hot day.

Similar phenomena have occurred hundreds of times since, in many houses and under various conditions. Sometimes the flowers have been in vast quantities, heaped upon the table. Often flowers or fruits asked for are brought. A friend of mine asked for a sunflower, and one six feet high fell upon the table, having a large mass of earth about its roots. One of the most striking tests was at Florence, with Mr. T. Adolphus Trollope, Mrs. Trollope, Miss Blagden, and Colonel Harvey. The room was searched by the gentlemen; Mrs. Guppy was undressed and redressed by Mrs. Trollope, every article of her clothing being examined. Mr. and Mrs. Guppy were both firmly held while at the table. In about ten minutes all the party exclaimed that they smelt flowers, and, on lighting a candle, both Mrs. Guppy's and Mr. Trollope's arms were found covered with jonquils, which filled the room with their odour. Mr. Guppy and Mr. Trollope both relate this in substantially the same terms. ("Dialectical Society's Report on Spiritualism," p and 372.)

Surely these are phenomena about which there can be no mistake. What theories have ever been proposed by our scientific teachers which even attempt to account for them? Delusion it cannot be, for the flowers are real, and can be preserved, and imposture under the conditions described is even less credible. If the gentlemen who came forward to enlighten the public on the subject of "so-called spiritual manifestations" do not know of the various classes of phenomena that have now been indicated, and the weight of the testimony in support of them, they are palpably unqualified for the task they have undertaken. That they do know of them, but keep back their knowledge, while putting forward trivialities easy to laugh at or expose, is a supposition I cannot for a moment entertain. Before leaving this part of the subject, it is well to note the fact of the marked individuality of each medium. They are not copies of each other, but each one develops a characteristic set of phenomena--a fact highly suggestive of some unconscious occult power in the individual, and wholly opposed to the idea of either imposture or delusion, both of which almost invariably copy pre-existing models.

Investigations by some Notable Sceptics.--In giving some account of how a few of the more important converts to Spiritualism became convinced, we are of course limited to those who have given their experiences to the public. I will first take the case of the eminent American lawyer, the Honourable J. W. Edmunds, commonly called Judge Edmunds; and it may be as well to let English sceptics know what he is thought of by his countrymen. When he first became a spiritualist he was greatly abused; and it was even declared that he consulted the spirits on his judicial decisions. To defend himself, he published an "Appeal to the Public," giving a full account of the inquiries which resulted in his conversion. In noticing this, the New York *Evening Mirror* said: "John W. Edmunds, the Chief Justice of the Supreme Court of this District, is an able lawyer, an industrious judge, and a good citizen. For the last eight years occupying without interruption the highest judicial stations, whatever may be his faults, no one can justly accuse him of a lack of ability, industry, honesty, or fearlessness. No one can doubt his general saneness, or can believe for a moment that the ordinary operations of his mind are not as rapid, accurate, and reliable as ever. Both by the practitioners and suitors at his bar, he is recognised as the head, in fact and in merit, of the Supreme Court for this District."A few years later he published a series of letters on Spiritualism in the *New York Tribune*; and in the first of these he gives a compact summary of his mode of investigation, from which the following passages are extracted. It must be remembered that at the time he commenced the inquiry he was in the prime and vigour of intellectual life, being fifty-two years of age.

"It was in January, 1851, that I first began my investigations, and it was not until April, 1853, that I became a firm believer in the reality of spiritual intercourse. During twenty-three months of those twenty-seven, I witnessed several hundred manifestations in various forms. I kept very minute and careful records of many of them. My practice was, whenever I attended a circle, to keep in pencil a memorandum of all that took place, so far as I could, and, as soon as I returned home, to write out a full account of what I had witnessed. I did all this with as much minuteness and particularity as I had ever kept any record of a trial before me in court. In this way, during that period, I preserved the record of nearly two hundred interviews, running through some one thousand six hundred pages of manuscript. I had these interviews with many different mediums, and under an infinite variety of circumstances. No two interviews were alike. There was always something new, or something different from what had previously occurred; and it very seldom happened that only the same persons were present. The manifestations were of almost every known form, physical or mental; sometimes only one, and sometimes both combined.

"I resorted to every expedient I could devise to detect imposture and to guard against delusion. I felt in myself, and saw in others, how exciting was the idea that we were actually communing with the dead; and I laboured to prevent any undue bias of my judgment. I was at times critical and captious to an unreasonable extreme; and when my belief was challenged, as it was over and over again, I refused to yield, except to evidence that would leave no possible room for cavil.

"I was severely exacting in my demands, and this would frequently happen. I would go to a circle with some doubt on my mind as to the manifestations at the previous circle, and something would happen aimed directly at that doubt, and completely overthrowing it as it then seemed, so that I had no longer any reason to doubt. But I would go home and write out carefully my minutes of the evening, cogitate over them for several days, compare them with previous records, and finally find some loophole--some possibility that it might have been something else than spiritual influence, and I would go to the next circle with a new doubt, and a new set of queries."

"I look back sometimes now, with a smile, at the ingenuity I wasted in devising ways and means to avoid the possibility of deception."

"It was a remarkable feature of my investigations, that every conceivable objection I could raise was, first or last, met and answered."

The following extracts are from the "Appeal":--

"I have seen a mahogany table, having a centre leg, and with a lamp burning upon it, lifted from the floor at least a foot, in spite of the efforts of those present, and shaken backward and forward as one would shake a goblet in his hand, and the lamp retain its place, though its glass pendants rang again."

"I have known a mahogany chair thrown on its side and moved swiftly back and forth on the floor, no one touching it, through a room where there were at least a dozen people sitting, yet no one was touched; and it was repeatedly stopped within a few inches of me, when it was coming with a violence which, if not arrested, must have broken my legs."

Having satisfied himself of the reality of the physical phenomena, he came to the question of whence comes the intelligence that was so remarkably connected with them.

He says:--

"Preparatory to meeting a circle, I have sat down alone in my room, and carefully prepared a series of questions to be propounded, and I have been surprised to find my questions answered, and in the precise order in which I wrote them, without my even taking my memorandum out of my pocket, and when not a person present knew that I had prepared questions, much less what they were. My most secret thoughts, those which I have never uttered to mortal man or woman, have been freely spoken to as if I had uttered them; and I have been admonished that my every thought was known to, and could be disclosed by, the intelligence which was thus manifesting itself."

"Still the question occurred, 'May not all this have been, by some mysterious operation, the mere reflex of the mind of some one present?' The answer was, that facts were communicated which were unknown then, but afterwards found to be true; like this, for instance: when I was absent last winter in Central America, my friends in town heard of my whereabouts and of the state of my health several times; and on my return, by comparing their information with the entries in my journal, it was found to be invariably correct. So thoughts have been uttered on subjects not then in my mind and utterly at variance with my own notions. This has often happened to me and to others, so as fully to establish the fact that it was not our minds that gave forth or affected the communication."

These few extracts sufficiently show that the writer was aware of the possible sources of error in such an inquiry; and the details given in the letters prove that he was constantly on his guard against them. He himself and his daughter became mediums; so that he afterwards obtained personal confirmation of many of the phenomena by himself alone. But all the phenomena referred to in the letters and "Appeal" occurred to him in the presence of others, who testified to them as well, and thus removed the possibility that the phenomena were subjective.

We have yet to add a notice of what will be perhaps, to many persons, the most startling and convincing of all the Judge's experiences. His own daughter became a medium for speaking foreign languages of which she was totally ignorant. He says: "She knows no language but her own, and a little smattering of boarding-school French; yet she has spoken in nine or ten different tongues, often for an hour at a time, with the ease and fluency of a native. It is not infrequent that foreigners converse with their spirit-friends through her, in their own language." One of these cases must be given.

"One evening, when some twelve or fifteen persons were in my parlour, Mr. E. D. Green, an artist of this city, was shown in accompanied by a gentleman whom he introduced as Mr. Evangelides, of Greece. Ere long a spirit spoke to him through Laura, in English, and said so many things to him that he identified him as a friend who had died at his house a few years before, but of whom none of us had ever heard. Occasionally, through Laura, the spirit would speak a word or a sentence in Greek, until Mr. E. inquired if he could be understood if he spoke Greek? The residue of the conversation for more than an hour was, on his part, entirely in Greek, and on hers sometimes in Greek and sometimes in English. At times Laura would not understand what was the idea conveyed either by her or him. At other times she would understand him, though he spoke in Greek, and herself, while uttering Greek words."

Several other cases are mentioned, and it is stated that this lady has spoken Spanish, French, Greek, Italian, Portuguese, Latin, Hungarian and Indian; and other languages which were unknown to any person present.

This is by no means an isolated case, but it is given as being on most unexceptionable authority. A man must know whether his own daughter has learnt, so as to speak fluently, eight languages besides her own, or not. Those who carry on the conversation must know whether the language is spoken, or not; and in several cases--as the Latin, Spanish, and Indian--the judge himself understood the language. And the phenomenon is connected with Spiritualism by the speaking being in the name of, and purporting to come from, some deceased person, and the subject matter being characteristic of that person. Such a case as this, which has been published sixteen years, ought to have been noticed and explained by those who profess to enlighten the public on the subject of Spiritualism.

Our next example is one of the most recent, but at the same time one of the most useful, converts to the truths of Spiritualism. Dr. George Sexton, M.D., M.A., L.L.D., was for many years the coadjutor of Mr. Bradlaugh, and one of the most earnest and energetic of the secularist teachers. The celebrated Robert Owen first called his attention to the subject of Spiritualism about twenty years ago. He read books, he saw a good deal of the ordinary physical manifestations, but he always "suspected that the mediums played tricks, and that the whole affair was nothing but clever conjuring by means of concealed machinery." He gave several lectures against Spiritualism in the usual style of non-believers, dwelling much on the absurdity and triviality of the phenomena, and ridiculing the idea that they were the work of spirits. Then came another old friend and fellow-secularist, Mr. Turley, who, after investigating the subject for the purpose of exposing it, became a firm believer. Dr. Sexton laughed at this conversion, yet it made a deep impression on his mind. Ten years passed away, and his next important investigation was with the Davenport brothers; and it will be well for those who sneer at these much-abused young men to take note of the following account of Dr. Sexton's proceedings with them, and especially of the fact that they cheerfully submitted to every test the doctor suggested. He tells us (in his lecture, "How I became a Spiritualist") that he visited them again and again, trying in vain to find out the trick. Then, he says--

"My partner--Dr. Barker--and I invited the Brothers to our houses, and, in order to guard against anything like trickery, we requested them not to bring any ropes, instruments, or other apparatus; all these we ourselves had determined to supply. Moreover, as there were four of them, viz., the two Brothers Davenport, Mr. Fay, and Dr. Fergusson, we suspected that the two who were not tied might really do all that was done. We therefore requested only two to come. They unhesitatingly complied with all these requests. We formed a circle, consisting entirely of members of our own families and a few private friends, with the one bare exception of Mrs. Fay. In the circle we all joined hands, and as Mrs. Fay sat at one end she had one of her hands free, while I had hold of the other. Thinking that she might be able to assist with the hand that was thus free, I asked as a favour that I might be allowed to hold both her hands--a proposition which she at once agreed to. Now, without entering here at all into what took place, suffice it to say that we bound the mediums with our own ropes, placed their feet upon sheets of writing paper and drew lines around their boots, so that if they moved their feet it should be impossible for them to place them again in the same position; we laid pence on their toes, sealed the ropes, and in every way took precautions against their moving. On the occasion to which I now refer, Mr. Bradlaugh and Mr. Charles Watts were present; and when Mr. Fay's coat had been taken off, the ropes still remaining on his hands, Mr. Bradlaugh requested that his coat might be placed on Mr. Fay, which was immediately done, the ropes still remaining fastened. We got on this occasion all the phenomena that usually occurred in the presence of these extraordinary men, particulars of which I shall probably give on another occasion. Dr. Barker became a believer in Spiritualism from the time that the Brothers visited at his house. I did not see that any proof had been given that disembodied spirits had any hand in producing the phenomena; but I was convinced that no tricks had been played, and that therefore these extraordinary physical manifestations were the result of some occult force in nature which I had no means of explaining in the present state of my knowledge. All the physical phenomena that I had seen now became clear to me; they were not accomplished by trickery, as I had formerly supposed, but were the result of some undiscovered law of nature which it was the business of the man of science to use his utmost endeavours to discover."

While he was maintaining this ground, spiritualists often asked him how he explained the intelligence that was manifested; and he invariably replied that he had not yet seen proofs of any intelligence other than what might be that of the medium or of some other persons present in the circle, adding, that as soon as he did see proofs of such intelligence he should become a spiritualist. In this position he stood for many years, till he naturally believed he should never see cause to change his opinion. He continued the inquiry, however, and in 1865 began to hold séances at home; but it was years before any mental phenomena occurred which were absolutely conclusive, although they were often of so startling a nature as would have satisfied any one less sceptical. At length, after fifteen years of enlightened scepticism--a scepticism not founded upon ignorance, but which refused to go one step beyond what the facts so diligently pursued absolutely demonstrated--the needful evidence came:--

"The proofs that I did ultimately receive are, many of them, of a character that I cannot describe minutely to a public audience, nor indeed have I time to do so. Suffice it to say, that I got in my own house, in the absence of all mediums other than those members of my own family and intimate private friends in whom mediumistic powers became developed, evidence of an irresistible character that the communications came from deceased friends and relatives. Intelligence was again and again displayed which could not possibly have had any other origin than that which it professed to have. Facts were named known to no one in the circle, and left to be verified afterwards. The identity of the spirits communicating was proved in a hundred different ways. Our dear departed ones made themselves palpable both to feeling and to sight; and the doctrine of spirit-communion was proved beyond the shadow of a doubt. I soon found myself in the position of Dr. Fenwick in Lord Lytton's 'Strange Story.' 'Do you believe,' asked the female attendant of Margrave, 'in that which you seek?' 'I have no belief,' was the answer. 'True science has none; true science questions all things, and takes nothing on credit. It knows but three states of mind--denial, conviction, and the vast interval between the two, which is not belief, but the suspension of judgment.' This describes exactly the phases through which my mind has passed."

Since Dr. Sexton has become a spiritualist he has been as energetic an advocate for its truths as he had been before for the negations of secularism. His experience and ability as a lecturer, with his long schooling in every form of manifestation, render him one of the most valuable promulgators of its teachings. He has also done excellent service in exposing the pretensions of those conjurors who profess to expose Spiritualism. This he does in the most practical way, not only by explaining how the professed imitations of spiritual manifestations are performed, but by actually performing them before his audience; and at the same time pointing out the important differences between what these people do and what occurs at good séances. Any one who wishes to comprehend how Dr. Lynn, Messrs. Maskelyne and Cook, and Herr Dobler perform some of their most curious feats have only to read his lecture, entitled, "Spirit Mediums and Conjurors," before going to witness their entertainments. We can hardly believe that the man who does this, and who during fifteen years of observation and experiment held out against the spiritual theory, is one of those who, as Lord Amberley tells us, "fall a victim to the most patent frauds, and are imposed upon by jugglery of the most vulgar order;" or who, as viewed from Professor Tyndall's high scientific standpoint, are in a frame of mind before which science is utterly powerless--"dupes beyond the reach of proof, who like to believe and do not like to be undeceived." These be brave words; but we leave our readers to judge whether they come with a very good grace from men who have the most slender and inadequate knowledge of the subject they are criticising, and no knowledge at all of the long-continued and conscientious investigations of many who are included in their wholesale animadversions.

Yet one more witness to these marvellous phenomena we must bring before our readers--a trained and experienced physicist, who has experimented in his own laboratory, and has applied tests and measurements of the most rigid and conclusive character. When Mr. Crookes--the discoverer of the metal thallium, and a Fellow of the Royal Society--first announced that he was going to investigate so-called spiritual phenomena, many public writers were all approval; for the complaint had long been that men of science were not permitted by mediums to inquire too scrupulously into the facts. One expressed "profound satisfaction that the subject was about to be investigated by a man so well qualified;" another was "gratified to learn that the matter is now receiving the attention of cool and clear-headed men of recognised position in science;" while a third declared that "no one could doubt Mr. Crookes's ability to conduct the investigation with rigid philosophical impartiality." But these expressions were evidently insincere, and were only meant to apply, in case the result was in accordance with the writers' notions of what it ought to be. Of course, a "scientific investigation" would explode the whole thing. Had not Faraday exploded table-turning? They hailed Mr. Crookes as the Daniel come to judgment--as the prophet who would curse their enemy, Spiritualism, by detecting imposture and illusion. But when the judge, after a patient trial lasting several years, decided against them, and their accepted prophet blessed the hated thing as an undoubted truth, their tone changed; and they began to suspect the judge's ability, and to pick holes in the evidence on which he founded his judgment.

In Mr. Crookes's latest paper, published in the *Quarterly Journal of Science* for January last, we are informed that he has pursued the inquiry for four years; and besides attending séances elsewhere, has had the opportunity of making numerous experiments in his own house with the two remarkable mediums already referred to, Mr. D. D. Home and Miss Kate Fox. These experiments were almost exclusively made in the light, under conditions of his own arranging, and with his own friends as witnesses. Such phenomena as percussive sounds; alteration of the weight of bodies; the rising of heavy bodies in the air without contact by any one; the levitation of human beings; luminous appearances of various kinds; the appearance of hands which lift small objects, yet are not the hands of any one present; direct writing by a luminous detached hand or by the pencil alone; phantom forms and faces; and various mental phenomena--have all been tested so variously and so repeatedly that Mr. Crookes is thoroughly satisfied of their objective reality. These phenomena are given in outline in the paper above referred to, and they will be detailed in full in a volume now preparing. I will not, therefore, weary my readers by repeating them here, but will remark, that these experiments have a weight as evidence vastly greater than would be due to them as resting on the testimony of any man of science, however distinguished, because they are, in almost every case, confirmations of what previous witnesses in immense numbers have testified to, in various places, and under various conditions, during the last twenty years. In every other experimental inquiry, without exception, confirmation of the facts of an earlier observer is held to add so greatly to their value, that no one treats them with the same incredulity with which he might have received them the first time they were announced. And when the confirmation has been repeated by three or four independent observers under favourable conditions, and there is nothing but theory or negative evidence against them, the facts are admitted--at least provisionally, and until disproved by a greater weight of evidence or by discovering the exact source of the fallacy of preceding observers.

But here, a totally different--a most unreasonable and a most unphilosophical--course is pursued. Each fresh observation, confirming previous evidence, is treated as though it were now put forth for the *first* time; and fresh confirmation is asked of it. And when this fresh and independent confirmation comes, yet more confirmation is asked for, and so on without end. This is a very clever way to ignore and stifle a new truth; but the facts of Spiritualism are ubiquitous in their occurrence and of so indisputable a nature, as to compel conviction in every earnest inquirer. It thus happens that although every fresh convert requires a large proportion of the series of demonstrative facts to be reproduced before he will give his assent to them, the number of such converts has gone on steadily increasing for a quarter of a century. Clergymen of all sects, literary men and lawyers, physicians in large numbers, men of science not a few, secularists, philosophical sceptics, pure materialists, all have become converts through the overwhelming logic of the phenomena which Spiritualism has brought before them. And what have we *per contra*? Neither science nor philosophy, neither scepticism nor religion, has ever yet in this quarter of a century made one single convert from the ranks of Spiritualism! This being the case, and fully appreciating the amount of candour and fairness, and knowledge of the subject, that has been exhibited by their opponents, is it to be wondered at that a large proportion of spiritualists are now profoundly indifferent to the opinion of men of science, and would not go one step out of their way to convince them? They say, that the movement is going on quite fast enough. That it is spreading by its own inherent force of truth, and slowly permeating all classes of society. It has thriven in spite of abuse and persecution, ridicule and argument, and will continue to thrive whether endorsed by great names or not. Men of science, like all others, are welcome to enter its ranks; but they must satisfy themselves by their own persevering researches, not expect to have its proofs laid before them. Their rejection of its truths is their own loss, but cannot in the slightest degree affect the progress of Spiritualism. The attacks and criticisms of the press are borne good-humouredly, and seldom excite other feelings than pity for the wilful ignorance and contempt for the overwhelming presumption of their writers. Such are the sentiments that are continually expressed by spiritualists; and it is as well, perhaps, that the outer world, to whom the literature of the movement is as much unknown as the Vedas, should be made acquainted with them.

Investigation by the Dialectical Committee.--There are many other investigators who ought to be noticed in any complete sketch of the subject, but we have now only space to allude briefly to the "Report of the Committee of the Dialectical Society." Of this committee, consisting of thirty-three acting members, only eight were, at the commencement, believers in the reality of the phenomena, while not more than four accepted the spiritual theory. During the course of the inquiry at least twelve of the complete sceptics became convinced of the reality of many of the physical phenomena through attending the experimental sub-committees, and almost wholly by means of the mediumship of members of the committee. At least three members who were previously sceptics pursued their investigations outside the committee meetings, and in consequence have become thorough spiritualists. My own observation, as a member of the committee and of the largest and most active sub-committee, enables me to state that the degree of conviction produced in the minds of the various members was, allowing for marked differences of character, approximately proportionate to the amount of time and care bestowed on the investigation. This fact, which is what occurs in all investigation into these phenomena, is a characteristic result of the examination into any natural phenomena. The examination into an imposture or delusion has, invariably, exactly opposite results; those who have slender experience being deceived, while those who perseveringly continue the inquiry inevitably find out the source of the deception or the delusion. If this were not so, the discovery of truth and the detection of error would be alike impossible. The result of this inquiry on the members of the committee themselves is, therefore, of more importance than the actual phenomena they witnessed, since these were far less striking than many of the facts already mentioned. But they are also of importance as confirming, by a body of intelligent and unprejudiced men, the results obtained by previous individual inquirers.

Before leaving this report, I must call attention to the evidence it furnishes of the state of opinion among men of education in France. M. Camille Flammarion, the well-known astronomer, sent a communication to the committee which deserves special consideration. Besides declaring his own acceptance of the objective reality of the phenomena after ten years of investigation, he makes the following statement:--

"My learned teacher and friend, M. Babinet, of the Institute, who has endeavoured, with M. E. Liais (now Director of the Observatory of Brazil), and several others of my colleagues of the Observatory of Paris, to ascertain their nature and cause, is not fully convinced of the intervention of spirits in their production; though this hypothesis, by which alone certain categories of these phenomena would seem to be explicable, has been adopted by many of our most esteemed *savants*, among others by Dr. Hoffle, the learned author of the 'History of Chemistry' and the 'General Encyclopædia;' and by the diligent labourer in the field of astronomic discovery whose death we have recently had to deplore, M. Hermann Goldschmidt, the discoverer of fourteen planets."

It thus appears that in France, as well as in America and in this country, men of science of no mean rank have investigated these phenomena and have found them to be realities; while some of the most eminent hold the spiritual theory to be the only one that will explain them.

This seems the proper place to notice the astounding assertion of certain writers, that there is not "a particle of evidence" to support the spiritual theory; that those who accept it betray "hopeless inability to discriminate between adequate and inadequate proof of facts;" that the theory is "formed apart from facts;" and, that those who accept it are so unable to reason, as to "jump to the conclusion" that it must be spirits that move tables, merely because they do not know how else they can be moved. The preceding account of how converts to Spiritualism have been made is a sufficient answer to all this ignorant assertion. The spiritual theory, as a rule, has only been adopted as a last resource, when all other theories have hopelessly broken down; and when fact after fact, phenomenon after phenomenon, has presented itself, giving direct proof that the so-called dead are still alive. The spiritual theory is the logical outcome of the whole of the facts. Those who deny it, in every instance with which I am acquainted, either from ignorance or disbelief leave half the facts out of view. Take the one case (out of many almost equally conclusive) of Mr. Livermore, who during five years, on hundreds of occasions, saw, felt, and heard the movements of the figure of his dead wife in absolute, unmistakable, living form. A form which could move objects, and which repeatedly wrote to him in her own handwriting and her own language, on cards which remained after the figure had disappeared. A form which was equally visible and tangible to two friends; which appeared in his own house, in a room absolutely secured, with the presence of only a young girl, the medium. Had these three men "not a particle of evidence" for the spiritual theory? Is it, in fact, possible to conceive or suggest any more complete proof? The facts must be got rid of before you can abolish the theory; and simple denial or disbelief does not get rid of facts testified during a space of five years by three witnesses, all men in responsible positions, and carrying on their affairs during the whole period in a manner to win the respect and confidence of their fellow citizens.[3]

Alfred R. Wallace.

(To be concluded in the next Number.)

Notes Appearing in the Original Work

1. The following are the more important works which have been used in the preparation of this article:--Judge Edmond's "Spiritual Tracts," New York, 1858-1860. Robert Dale Owen's "Footfalls on the Boundary of Another World," Trübner and Co., 1861. E. Hardinge's "Modern American Spiritualism," New York, 1870. Robert Dale Owen's "Debateable Land between this World and the Next," Trübner and Co., 1871. "Report on Spiritualism of the Committee of the London Dialectical Society," Longmans and Co., 1871. "Year Book of Spiritualism," Boston and London, 1871. Hudson Tuttle's "Arcana of Spiritualism," Boston, 1871. *The Spiritual Magazine*, 1861-1874. *The Spiritualist Newspaper*, 1872-1874. *The Medium and Daybreak*, 1869-1874. on

2. It may be as well here to explain that the word "spirit," which is often considered to be so objectionable by scientific men, is used throughout this article (or at all events in the earlier portions of it) merely to avoid circumlocution, in the sense of the "intelligent cause of the phenomena," and not as implying "the spirits of the dead," unless so expressly stated. on

3. The objection will here inevitably be made: "These wonderful things always happen in America. When they occur in England it will be time enough to inquire into

them." Singularly enough, after this article was in the press the final test was obtained, which demonstrated the occurrence of similar phenomena in London. A short statement may, therefore, be interesting for those who cannot digest American evidence. For some years a young lady, Miss Florence Cook, has exhibited remarkable mediumship, which latterly culminated in the production of an entire female form purporting to be spiritual, and which appeared barefooted and in white flowing robes while she lay entranced, in dark clothing and securely bound, in a cabinet or adjacent room. Notwithstanding that tests of an apparently conclusive character were employed, many visitors, spiritualists as well as sceptics, got the impression that all was not as it should be; owing in part to the resemblance of the supposed spirit to Miss Cook, and also to the fact that the two could not be seen at the same time. Some supposed that Miss C. was an impostor who managed to conceal a white robe about her (although she was often searched), and who, although she was securely tied with tapes and sealed, was able to get out of her bonds, dress and undress herself, and get into them again, all in the dark, and in so complete and skilful manner as to defy detection. Others thought that the spirit released her, provided her with a white dress, and sent her forth to personate a ghost. The belief that there was something wrong led one gentleman--an ardent spiritualist--to seize the supposed spirit and endeavour to hold it, in the hope that some other person would open the cabinet-door and see if Miss Cook was really there. This was, unfortunately, not done; but the great resemblance of the being he seized to Miss Cook, its perfect solidity, and the vigorous struggles it made to escape from him, convinced this gentleman that it was Miss Cook herself, although the rest of the company, a few minutes afterwards, found her bound and sealed just as she had been left an hour before. To determine the question conclusively, experiments have been made within the last few weeks by two scientific men, Mr. C. F. Varley, F.R.S., the eminent electrician, made use of a galvanic battery and cable-testing apparatus, and passed a current through Miss Cook's body (by fastening sovereigns soldered to wires to her arms). The apparatus was so delicate that any movement whatever was instantly indicated, while it was impossible for the young lady to dress and act as a ghost without breaking the circuit. Yet under these conditions the spirit-form did appear, exhibited its arms, spoke, wrote, and touched several persons; and this happened, be it remembered, not in the medium's own house, but in that of a private gentleman in the West End of London. For nearly an hour the circuit was never broken, and at the conclusion Miss Cook was found in a deep trance. Since this remarkable experiment Mr. William Crookes, F.R.S., has obtained, if possible, still more satisfactory evidence. He contrived a phosphorus lamp, and armed with this was allowed to go into the dark room accompanied by the spirit, and there saw and felt Miss Cook, dressed in black velvet, lying in a trance on the floor, while the spirit-form, in white robes, stood close beside her. During the evening this spirit-form had been, for nearly an hour, walking and talking with the company; and Mr. Crookes, by permission, clasped the figure in his arms, and found it to be, apparently, a real living woman, just as the sceptical gentleman had done. Yet this figure is not that of Miss Cook, nor of any other human being, since it appeared and disappeared in Mr. Crookes's own house as completely as in that of the medium herself. The full statements of Messrs. Varley and Crookes, with a mass of interesting detail on the subject, appeared in the *Spiritualist* newspaper in March and April last; and they serve to show that whatever marvels occur in America can be reproduced here, and that men of science are not precluded from investigating these phenomena with scientific instruments and by scientific methods. In the concluding part of this paper we shall be able to show that another class of manifestation which originated in America--that of the so-called spirit-photographs--has been first critically examined and completely demonstrated in our own country.   on

* * *

A DEFENCE OF MODERN SPIRITUALISM.

PART II.
SPIRIT-PHOTOGRAPHS.

We now approach a subject which cannot be omitted in any impartial sketch of the evidences of Spiritualism, since it is that which furnishes perhaps the most unassailable demonstration it is possible to obtain, of the objective reality of spiritual forms, and also of the truthful nature of the evidence furnished by seers when they describe figures visible to themselves alone. It has been already indicated-- and it is a fact, of which the records of Spiritualism furnish ample proof--that different individuals possess the power of seeing such forms and figures in very variable degrees. Thus, it often happens at a séance, that some will see distinct lights of which they will describe the form, appearance, and position, while others will see nothing at all. If only one or two persons see the lights, the rest will naturally impute it to their imagination; but there are cases in which only one or two of those present are unable to see them. There are also cases in which all see them, but in very different degrees of distinctness; yet that they see the same objects is proved by their all agreeing as to the position and the movement of the lights. Again, what some see as merely luminous clouds, others will see as distinct human forms, either partial or entire. In other cases all present see the form--whether hand, face, or entire figure--with equal distinctness. Again, the objective reality of these appearances is sometimes proved by their being touched, or by their being seen to move objects,--in some cases heard to speak, in others seen to write, by several persons at one and the same time; the figure seen or the writing produced being sometimes unmistakably recognisable as that of some deceased friend. A volume could easily be filled with records of this class of appearances, authenticated by place, date, and names of witnesses; and a considerable selection is to be found in the works of Mr. Robert Dale Owen.

Now, at this point, an inquirer, who had not pre-judged the question, and who did not believe his own knowledge of the universe to be so complete as to justify him in rejecting all evidence for facts which he had hitherto considered to be in the highest degree improbable, might fairly say, "Your evidence for the appearance of visible, tangible, spiritual forms, is very strong; but I should like to have them submitted to a crucial test, which would quite settle the question of the possibility of their being due to a coincident delusion of several senses of several persons at the same time; and, if satisfactory, would demonstrate their objective reality in a way nothing else can do. If they really reflect or emit light which makes them visible to human eyes, *they can be photographed*. Photograph them, and you will have an unanswerable proof that your human witnesses are trustworthy." Two years ago we could only have replied to this very proper suggestion, that we believed it had been done and could be again done, but that we had no satisfactory evidence to offer. Now, however, we are in a position to state, not only that it has been frequently done, but that the evidence is of such a nature as to satisfy any one who will take the trouble carefully to examine it. This evidence we will now lay before our readers, and we venture to think they will acknowledge it to be most remarkable.

Before doing so it may be as well to clear away a popular misconception. Mr. Lewes advised the Dialectical Committee to distinguish carefully between "facts and inferences from facts." This is especially necessary in the case of what are called spirit-photographs. The figures which occur in these, when not produced by any human agency, may be of "spiritual" origin, without being figures "of spirits." There is much evidence to show that they are, in some cases, forms produced by invisible intelligences, but distinct from them. In other cases the intelligence appears to clothe itself with matter capable of being perceived by us; but even then it does not follow that the form produced is the actual image of the spiritual form. It may be but a reproduction of the former mortal form with its terrestrial accompaniments, *for purposes of recognition.*

Most persons have heard of these "ghost-pictures," and how easily they can be made to order by any photographer, and are therefore disposed to think they can be of no use as evidence. But a little consideration will show them that the means by which sham ghosts can be manufactured being so well known to all photographers, it becomes easy to apply tests or arrange conditions so as to prevent imposition. The following are some of the more obvious:--

1. If a person with a knowledge of photography takes his own glass plates, examines the camera used and all the accessories, and watches the whole process of taking a picture, then, if any definite form appears on the negative besides the sitter, it is a proof that some object was present capable of reflecting or emitting the actinic rays, although invisible to those present. 2. If an unmistakable likeness appears of a deceased person totally unknown to the photographer. 3. If figures appear on the negative having a definite relation to the figure of the sitter, who chooses his own position, attitude, and accompaniments, it is a proof that invisible figures were really there. 4. If a figure appears draped in white, and partly behind the dark body of the sitter without in the least showing through, it is a proof that the white

figure was there at the same time, because the dark parts of the negative are transparent, and any white picture in any way superposed would show through. 5. Even should none of these tests be applied, yet if a medium, quite independent of the photographer, sees and describes a figure during the sitting, and an exactly corresponding figure appears on the plate, it is a proof that such a figure was there.

Every one of these tests have now been successfully applied in our own country, as the following outline of the facts will show.

The accounts of spirit-photography in several parts of the United States caused many spiritualists in this country to make experiments; but for a long time without success. Mr. and Mrs. Guppy, who are both amateur photographers, tried at their own house, and failed. In March, 1872, they went one day to Mr. Hudson's, a photographer living near them (not a spiritualist) to get some *cartes de visite* of Mrs. Guppy. After the sitting the idea suddenly struck Mr. Guppy that he would try for a spirit-photograph. He sat down, told Mrs. G. to go behind the background, and had a picture taken. There came out behind him a large, indefinite, oval, white patch, somewhat resembling the outline of a draped figure. Mrs. Guppy, behind the background, was dressed in black. This is the first spirit-photograph taken in England, and it is perhaps more satisfactory on account of the suddenness of the impulse under which it was taken, and the great white patch which no impostor would have attempted to produce, and which taken by itself, utterly spoils the picture. A few days afterwards, Mr. and Mrs. Guppy and their little boy went without any notice. Mrs. Guppy sat on the ground holding the boy on a stool. Her husband stood behind looking on. The picture thus produced is most remarkable. A tall female figure, finely draped in white, gauzy robes, stands directly behind and above the sitters, looking down on them and holding its open hands over their heads, as if giving a benediction. The face is somewhat Eastern, and, with the hands, is beautifully defined. The white robes pass behind the sitters' dark figures without in the least showing through. A second picture was then taken as soon as a plate could be prepared; and it was fortunate it was so, for it resulted in a most remarkable test. Mrs. Guppy again knelt with the boy; but this time she did not stoop so much, and her head was higher. The same white figure comes out equally well defined, but *it has changed its position in a manner exactly corresponding to the slight change of Mrs. Guppy's position.* The hands were before on a level; now one is raised considerably higher than the other, so as to keep it about the same distance from Mrs. Guppy's head as it was before. The folds of the drapery all correspondingly differ, and the head is slightly turned. Here, then, one of two things is absolutely certain. Either there was a living, intelligent, but invisible being present, or Mr. and Mrs. Guppy, the photographer, and some fourth person, planned a wicked imposture, and have maintained it ever since. Knowing Mr. and Mrs. Guppy so well as I do, I feel an absolute conviction that they are as incapable of an imposture of this kind as any earnest inquirer after truth in the department of natural science.

The report of these pictures soon spread. Spiritualists in great numbers came to try for similar results, with varying degrees of success; till after a time rumour of imposture arose, and it is now firmly believed by many, from suspicious appearances on the pictures and from other circumstances, that a large number of shams have been produced. It is certainly not to be wondered at if it be so. The photographer, remember, was not a spiritualist, and was utterly puzzled at the pictures above described. Scores of persons came to him, and he saw that they were satisfied if they got a second figure with themselves, and dissatisfied if they did not. He *may* have made arrangements by which to satisfy everybody. One thing is clear; that if there has been imposture, it was at once detected by spiritualists themselves; if not, then spiritualists have been quick in noticing what appeared to indicate it. Those, however, who most strongly assert imposture allow that a large number of genuine pictures have been taken. But, true or not, the cry of imposture did good, since it showed the necessity for tests and for independent confirmation of the facts.

The test of clearly recognisable likenesses of deceased

friends has often been obtained. Mr. William Howitt, who went without previous notice, obtained likenesses of two sons, many years dead, and of the very existence of one of which even the friend who accompanied Mr. Howitt was ignorant. The likenesses were instantly recognised by Mrs. Howitt; and Mr. Howitt declares them to be "perfect and unmistakable." (*Spiritual Magazine*, Oct., 1872.) Dr. Thomson of Clifton, obtained a photograph of himself, accompanied by that of a lady he did not know. He sent it to his uncle in Scotland, simply asking if he recognised a resemblance to any of the family deceased. The reply was that it was the likeness of Dr. Thomson's own mother, who died at his birth; and there being no picture of her in existence, he had no idea what she was like. The uncle very naturally remarked, that he "could not understand how it was done." (*Spiritual Magazine*, Oct., 1873.) Many other instances of recognition have occurred, but I will only add my personal testimony. A few weeks back I myself went to the same photographer's for the first time, and obtained a most unmistakable likeness of a deceased relative. We will now pass to a better class of evidence, the private experiments of amateurs.

Mr. Thomas Slater, an old-established optician in the Euston Road, and an amateur photographer, took with him to Mr. Hudson's, a new camera of his own manufacture and his own glasses, saw everything done, and obtained a portrait with a second figure on it. He then began experimenting in his own private house, and during last summer obtained some remarkable results. The first of his successes contains two heads by the side of a portrait of his sister. One of these heads is unmistakably the late Lord Brougham's; the other, much less distinct, is recognised by Mr. Slater as that of Robert Owen, whom he knew intimately up to the time of his death. He has since obtained several excellent pictures of the same class. One in particular, shows a female in black and white flowing robes, standing by the side of Mr. Slater. In another the head and bust appears, leaning over his shoulder. The faces of these two are much alike, and other members of the family recognise them as likenesses of Mr. Slater's mother, who died when he was an infant. In another a pretty child figure, also draped, stands beside Mr. Slater's little boy. Now, whether these figures are correctly identified or not, is not the essential point. The fact that *any* figures, so clear and unmistakably human in appearance as these, should appear on plates taken in his own private studio by an experienced optician and amateur photographer, who makes all his apparatus himself, and with no one present but the members of his own family,--is the real marvel. In one case a second figure appeared on a plate with himself, taken by Mr. Slater when he was absolutely alone--by the simple process of occupying the sitter's chair after uncapping the camera. He and his family being themselves mediums, they require no extraneous assistance; and this may, perhaps, be the reason why he has succeeded so well. One of the most extraordinary pictures obtained by Mr. Slater is a full-length portrait of his sister, in which there is no second figure, but the sitter appears covered all over with a kind of transparent lace drapery, which on examination is seen to be wholly made up of shaded circles of different sizes, quite unlike any material fabric I have seen or heard of.

Mr. Slater has himself shown me all these pictures and explained the conditions under which they were produced. That they are not impostures is certain; and as the first independent confirmations of what had been previously obtained only through professional photographers, their value is inestimable.

A less successful, but not perhaps on that account less satisfactory confirmation has been obtained by another amateur, who, after eighteen months of experiment, obtained a partial success. Mr. R. Williams, M.A., Ph.D., of Hayward's Heath, succeeded last summer in obtaining three photographs, each with part of a human form besides the sitter, one having the features distinctly marked. Subsequently another was obtained, with a well-formed figure of a man standing at the side of the sitter, but while being developed, this figure faded away entirely. Mr. Williams assures me (in a letter) that in these experiments there was "no room for trick or for the production of these figures by any known means."

The editor of the *British Journal of Photography* has made experiments at Mr. Hudson's studio, taking his own collodion and new plates, and doing everything himself, yet there were "abnormal appearances" on the pictures although no distinct figures.

We now come to the valuable and conclusive experiments of Mr. John Beattie of Clifton, a retired photographer of twenty years experience, and of whom the above-mentioned editor says:--"Every one who knows Mr. Beattie will give him credit for being a thoughtful, skilful, and intelligent photographer, one of the last men in the world to be easily deceived, at least in matters relating to photography, and one quite incapable of deceiving others."

Mr. Beattie has been assisted in his researches by Dr. Thomson, an Edinburgh M.D., who has practised photography, as an amateur, for twenty-five years. They experimented at the studio of a friend, who was not a spiritualist (but who became a medium during the experiments), and had the services of a tradesman with whom they were well acquainted, as a medium. The whole of the photographic work was done by Messrs. Beattie and Thomson, the other two sitting at a small table. The pictures were taken in series of three, within a few seconds of each other, and several of these series were taken at each sitting. The figures produced are for the most part not human, but variously formed and shaded white patches, which in successive pictures change their form and develope as it were into a more perfect or complete type. Thus, one set of five begins with two white somewhat angular patches over the middle sitter, and ends with a rude but unmistakable white female figure, covering the larger part of the plate. The other three show intermediate states, indicating a continuous change of form from the first figure to the last. Another set (of four pictures) begins with a white vertical cylinder over the body of the medium, and a shorter one on his head. These change their form in the second and third, and in the last become laterally spread out into luminous masses resembling nebulæ. Another set of three is very curious. The first has an oblique flowing luminous patch from the table to the ground; in the second this has changed to a white serpentine column, ending in a point above the medium's head; in the third the column has become broader and somewhat double, with the curve in an opposite direction, and with a head-like termination. The change of the curvature may have some connection with a change in the position of the sitters, which is seen to have taken place between the second and the third of this set. There are two others, taken, like all the preceding, in 1872, but which the medium described during the exposure. The first, he said, was a thick white fog; and the picture came out all shaded white, with not a trace of any of the sitters. The other was described as a fog with a figure standing in it; and here a white human figure is alone seen in the almost uniform foggy surface. During the experiments made in 1873, the medium, *in every case*, minutely and correctly described the appearances which afterwards came out on the plate. In one there is a luminous rayed star of large size, with a human face faintly visible in the centre. This is the last of three in which the star developed, and the whole were accurately described by the medium. In another set of three, the medium first described,--"a light behind him, coming from the floor." The next,--"a light rising over another person's arms, coming from his own boot." The third,--"there is the same light, but now a column comes up through the table, and it is hot to my hands." Then he suddenly exclaimed,--"What a bright light up there! Can you not see it?" pointing to it with his hand. All this most accurately describes the three pictures, and in the last, the medium's hand is seen pointing to a white patch which appears overhead. There are other curious developments, the nature of which is already sufficiently indicated; but one very startling single picture must be mentioned. During the exposure one medium said he saw on the background a black figure, the other medium saw a light figure by the side of the black one. In the picture both these figures appear, the light one very faintly, the black one much more distinctly, of a gigantic size, with a massive coarse-featured face and long hair. (*Spiritual Magazine*, January and August, 1873, *Photographic News*, June 28th, 1872.)

Mr. Beattie has been so good as to send me for examination a complete set of these most extraordinary photographs, thirty-two in number, and has furnished me with any particulars I desired. I have described them as correctly as I am able; and Dr. Thomson has authorised me to use his name as confirming Mr. Beattie's account of the conditions under which they appeared. These experiments were not made without labour and perseverance. Sometimes twenty consecutive pictures produced absolutely nothing unusual. Hundreds have been taken, and more than half have been complete failures. But the successes have been well worth the labour. They demonstrate the fact that what a medium or sensitive sees (even where no one else sees anything) may often have an objective existence. They teach us that perhaps the bookseller, Nicolai of Berlin--whose case has been quoted *ad nauseam* as the type of a "spectral illusion"--saw real beings after all; and that, had photography been then discovered and properly applied, we might now have the portraits of the invisible men and women who crowded his room. They give us hints of a process by which the figures seen at séances may have to be gradually formed or developed, and enable us better to understand the statements repeatedly made by the communicating intelligences, that it is very difficult to produce definite visible and tangible forms, and that it can only be done under a rare combination of favourable conditions.

We find, then, that three amateur photographers working independently in different parts of England, separately confirm the fact of spirit-photography,--already demonstrated to the satisfaction of many who had tested it through professional photographers. The experiments of Mr. Beattie and Dr. Thomson are alone absolutely conclusive; and, taken in connection with those of Mr. Slater and Dr. Williams, and the test photographs, like those of Mrs. Guppy, establish as a scientific fact the objective existence of invisible human forms, and definite invisible actinic images. Before leaving the photographic phenomena we have to notice two curious points in connection with them. The actinic action of the spirit-forms is peculiar, and much more rapid than that of the light reflected from ordinary material forms; for the figures start out the moment the developing fluid touches them, while the figure of the sitter appears much later. Mr. Beattie noticed this throughout his experiments, and I was myself much struck with it when watching the development of three pictures recently taken at Mr. Hudson's. The second figure, though by no means bright, always came out long before any other part of the picture. The other singular thing is, the copious drapery in which these forms are almost always enveloped, so as to show only just what is necessary for recognition, of the face and figure. The explanation given of this is, that the human form is more difficult to materialise than drapery. The conventional "white-sheeted ghost" was not then all fancy, but had a foundation in fact,--a fact, too, of deep significance, dependent on the laws of a yet unknown chemistry.

Summary of the More Important Manifestations, Physical and Mental.

As we have not been able to give an account of many curious facts which occur with the various classes of mediums, the following catalogue of the more important and well-characterized phenomena may be useful. They may be grouped provisionally, as, Physical, or those in which material objects are acted on, or apparently material bodies produced; and, Mental, or those which consist in the exhibition by the medium of powers or faculties not possessed in the normal state.

The principal physical phenomena are the following:--

1. *Simple Physical Phenomena.*--Producing sounds of all kinds, from a delicate tick to blows like those of a heavy sledge-hammer. Altering the weight of bodies. Moving bodies without human agency. Raising bodies into the air. Conveying bodies to a distance out of and into closed rooms. Releasing mediums from every description of bonds, even from welded iron rings, as has happened in America.

2. *Chemical.*--Preserving from the effects of fire, as already detailed.

3. *Direct Writing and Drawing.*--Producing writing or

drawing on marked papers, placed in such positions that no human hand (or foot) can touch them. Sometimes, visibly to the spectators, a pencil rising up and writing or drawing apparently by itself. Some of the drawings in many colours have been produced on marked paper in from ten to twenty seconds, and the colours found wet. (See Mr. Coleman's evidence, in "Dialectical Report," , confirmed by Lord Borthwick, .) Mr. Thomas Slater of 136 Euston Road, is now obtaining communication in the following manner:--A bit of slate pencil an eighth of an inch long is laid on a table; a clean slate is laid over this, in a well-lighted room; the sound of writing is then heard, and in a few minutes a communication of considerable length is found distinctly written. At other times the slate is held between himself and another person, their other hands being joined. Some of these communications are philosophical discussions on the nature of spirit and matter, supporting the usual spiritual theory on this subject.

4. *Musical Phenomena.*--Musical instruments, of various kinds, played without human agency, from a hand-bell to a closed piano. With some mediums, and where the conditions are favourable, original musical compositions of a very high character are produced. This occurs with Mr. Home.

5. *Spiritual Forms.*--These are either luminous appearances, sparks, stars, globes of light, luminous clouds, &c.; or, hands, faces, or entire human figures, generally

covered with flowing drapery, except a portion of the face and hands. The human forms are often capable of moving solid objects, and are both visible and tangible to all present. In other cases they are only visible to seers, but when this is the case it sometimes happens that the seer describes the figure as lifting a flower or a pen, and others present see the flower or the pen apparently move by itself. In some cases they speak distinctly; in others the voice is heard by all, the form only seen by the medium. The flowing robes of these forms have in some cases been examined, and pieces cut off, which have in a short time melted away. Flowers are also brought, some of which fade away and vanish; others are real, and can be kept indefinitely. It must not be concluded that any of these forms are actual spirits; they are probably only temporary forms produced by spirits for purposes of test, or of recognition by their friends. This is the account invariably given of them by communications obtained in various ways; so that the objection once thought to be so crushing--that there can be no "ghosts" of clothes, armour, or walking-sticks--ceases to have any weight.

6. *Spiritual Photographs.*--These, as just detailed, demonstrate by a purely physical experiment the trustworthiness of the preceding class of observations.

We now come to the mental phenomena, of which the following are the chief:--

1. *Automatic Writing.*--The medium writes involuntarily;

often matter which he is not thinking about, does not expect, and does not like. Occasionally definite and correct information is given of facts of which the medium has not, nor ever had, any knowledge. Sometimes future events are accurately predicted. The writing takes place either by the hand or through a planchette. Often the handwriting changes. Sometimes it is written backwards, sometimes in languages the medium does not understand.

2. *Seeing, or Clairvoyance and Clairaudience.*--This is of various kinds. Some mediums see the forms of deceased persons unknown to them, and describe their peculiarities so minutely that their friends at once recognise them. They often hear voices, through which they obtain names, date, and place, connected with the individuals so described. Others read sealed letters in any language, and write appropriate answers.

3. *Trance-speaking.*--The medium goes into a more or less unconscious state, and then speaks, often on matters and in a style far beyond his own capacities. Thus, Serjeant Cox--no mean judge on a matter of literary style--says, "I have heard an uneducated barman, when in a state of trance, maintain a dialogue with a party of philosophers on 'Reason and Foreknowledge, Will and Fate,' and hold his own against them. I have put to him the most difficult questions in psychology, and received answers, always thoughtful, often full of wisdom, and invariably conveyed in choice

and elegant language. Nevertheless a quarter of an hour afterwards, when released from the trance, he was unable to answer the simplest query on a philosophical subject, and was even at a loss for sufficient language to express a commonplace idea" ("What am I?" vol. ii., .) That this is not overstated I can myself testify, from repeated observation of the same medium. And from other trance-speakers--such as Mrs. Hardinge, Mrs. Tappan, and Mr. Peebles--I have heard discourses which, for high and sustained eloquence, noble thoughts, and high moral purpose, surpassed the best efforts of any preacher or lecturer within my experience.

4. *Impersonation.*--This occurs during trance. The medium seems taken possession of by another being; speaks, looks and acts the character in a most marvellous manner; in some cases speaks foreign languages never even heard in the normal state; as in the case of Miss Edmonds, already given. When the influence is violent or painful, the effects are such as have been in all ages imputed to possession by evil spirits.

5. *Healing.*--There are various forms of this. Sometimes by mere laying on of hands, an exalted form of simple mesmeric healing. Sometimes, in the trance state, the medium at once discovers the hidden malady, and prescribes for it, often describing very exactly the morbid appearance of internal organs.

The purely mental phenomena are generally of no use

as evidence to non-spiritualists, except in those few cases where rigid tests can be applied; but they are so intimately connected with the physical series, and often so interwoven with them, that no one who has sufficient experience to satisfy him of the reality of the former, fails to see that the latter form part of the general system, and are dependent on the same agencies.

With the physical series the case is very different. They form a connected body of evidence, from the simplest to the most complex and astounding, every single component fact of which can be, and has been, repeatedly demonstrated by itself; while each gives weight and confirmation to all the rest. They have all, or nearly all, been before the world for twenty years; the theories and explanations of reviewers and critics do not touch them, or in any way satisfy any sane man who has repeatedly witnessed them; they have been tested and examined by sceptics of every grade of incredulity, men in every way qualified to detect imposture or to discover natural causes--trained physicists, medical men, lawyers, and men of business--but in every case the investigators have either retired baffled, or become converts.

There have, it is true, been some impostors who have attempted to imitate the phenomena; but such cases are few in number, and have been discovered by tests far less severe than those to which the genuine phenomena have been submitted over and over again; and a large proportion of these phenomena have never been imitated, because they are beyond successful imitation.

Now what do our leaders of public opinion say, when a scientific man of proved ability again observes a large portion of the more extraordinary phenomena, in his own house, under test conditions, and affirms their objective reality; and this not after a hasty examination, but after four years of research? Men "with heavy scientific appendages to their names" refuse to examine them when invited; the eminent society of which he is a fellow refuses to record them; and the press cries out that it wants better witnesses than Mr. Crookes, and that such facts want "confirmation" before they can be believed. But why more confirmation? And when again "confirmed," who is to confirm the confirmer? After the whole range of the phenomena had been before the world ten years, and had convinced sceptics by tens of thousands--sceptics, be it remembered, of common sense and more than common acuteness, Americans of all classes-- they were *confirmed* by the first chemist in America, Professor Robert Hare. Two years later they were again confirmed by the elaborate and persevering inquiries of one of the first American lawyers, Judge Edmonds. Then by another good chemist, Professor Mapes. In France the truth of the simpler physical phenomena was *confirmed* by Count A. de Gasparin in 1854; and since then French astronomers, mathematicians, and chemists of high rank have *confirmed* them. Professor

Thury of Geneva again *confirmed* them, in 1855. In our own country such men as Professor de Morgan, Dr. Lockhart Robertson, T. Adolphus Trollope, Dr. Robert Chambers, Serjeant Cox, Mr. C. F. Varley, as well as the sceptical Dialectical Committee, have independently *confirmed* large portions of them; and lastly comes Mr. William Crookes, F.R.S., with four years of research and unrestricted experiment with the two oldest and most remarkable mediums in the world, and again *confirms* almost the whole series! But even this is not all. Through an independent set of most competent observers we have the crucial test of photography; a witness which cannot be deceived, which has no preconceived opinions, which cannot register "subjective" impressions; a thoroughly scientific witness, who is admitted into our law courts, and whose testimony is good as against any number of recollections of what did happen or opinions as to what ought to and must have happened. And what have the other side brought against this overwhelming array of consistent and unimpeachable evidence? They have merely made absurd and inadequate suppositions, but have not disproved or explained away one weighty fact!

My position, therefore, is, that the phenomena of Spiritualism in their entirety do *not* require further confirmation. They are proved quite as well as any facts are proved in other sciences; and it is not denial or quibbling that can disprove any of them, but only fresh facts and accurate deductions from those facts. When the opponents of Spiritualism can give a record of their researches approaching in duration and completeness to those of its advocates; and when they can discover and show in detail, either how the phenomena are produced or how the many sane and able men here referred to have been deluded into a coincident belief that they have witnessed them; and when they can prove the correctness of their theory by producing a like belief in a body of equally sane and able unbelievers,--then, and not till then, will it be necessary for spiritualists to produce fresh confirmation of facts which are, and always have been, sufficiently real and indisputable to satisfy any honest and persevering inquirer.

This being the state of the case as regards evidence and proof, we are fully justified in taking the *facts* of modern Spiritualism (and with them the spiritual theory as the only tenable one) as being fully established. It only remains to give a brief account of the more important uses and teachings of Spiritualism.

Historical Teachings of Spiritualism.

The lessons which modern Spiritualism teaches may be classed under two heads. In the first place, we find that it gives a rational account of various phenomena in human history which physical science has been unable to explain, and has therefore rejected or ignored; and, in the second, we derive from it some definite information as to man's nature and destiny, and, founded on this, an ethical system of great practical efficacy. The following are some of the more important phenomena of history and of human nature which science cannot deal with, but which Spiritualism explains:--

1. It is no small thing that the spiritualist finds himself able to rehabilitate Socrates as a sane man, and his "demon" as an intelligent spiritual being who accompanied him through life,--in other words, a guardian spirit. The non-spiritualist is obliged to look upon one of the greatest men in human history, not only as subject all his life to a mental illusion, but as being so weak, foolish, or superstitious as never to discover that it was an illusion. He is obliged to disbelieve the fact asserted by contemporaries and by Socrates himself, that it forewarned him truly of dangers; and to hold that this noble man, this subtle reasoner, this religious sceptic, who was looked up to with veneration and love by the great men who were his pupils, was imposed upon by his own fancies, and never during a long life found out that they were fancies, and that their supposed monitions were as often wrong as right. It is a positive mental relief not to have to think thus of Socrates.

2. Spiritualism allows us to believe that the oracles of antiquity were not all impostures; that a whole people, perhaps the most intellectually acute who ever existed, were not all dupes. In discussing the question, "Why the

Prophetess Pythia giveth no Answers now from the Oracle in Verse," Plutarch tells us that when kings and states consulted the oracle on weighty matters that might do harm if made public, the replies were couched in enigmatical language; but when private persons asked about their own affairs they got direct answers in the plainest terms, so that some people even complained of their simplicity and directness, as being unworthy of a divine origin. And he adds this positive testimony: "Her answers, though submitted to the severest scrutiny, have never proved false or incorrect. On the contrary, the verification of them has filled the temple with gifts from all parts of Greece and foreign countries." And again, "The answer of the Pythoness proceeds to the very truth, without any diversion, circuit, fraud, or ambiguity. It has never yet, in a single instance, been convicted of falsehood." Would such statements be made by such a writer, if these oracles were all the mere guesses of impostors? The fact that they declined and ultimately failed, is wholly in their favour; for why should imposture cease as the world became less enlightened and more superstitious? Neither does the fact that the priests could sometimes be bribed to give out false oracles prove anything, against such statements as that of Plutarch and the belief during many generations, supported by ever-recurring experiences, of the greatest men of antiquity. That belief could only have been formed by demonstrative facts; and modern Spiritualism enables us to understand the nature of those facts.

3. Both the Old and the New Testaments are full of Spiritualism, and spiritualists alone can read the record with an enlightened belief. The hand that wrote upon the wall at Belshazzar's feast, and the three men unhurt in Nebuchadnezzar's fiery furnace, are for them actual facts which they need not explain away. St. Paul's language about "spiritual gifts," and "trying the spirits," is to them intelligible language, and the "gift of tongues" a simple fact. When Christ cast out "devils" or evil spirits, he really did so--not merely startle a madman into momentary quiescence; and the water changed into wine, as well as the bread and fishes continually renewed till five thousand men were fed, are credible as extreme manifestations of a power which is still daily at work among us.

4. The miracles of the saints, when well attested, come into the same category. Those of St. Bernard, for instance, were often performed in broad day before thousands of spectators, and were recorded by eye-witnesses. He was himself greatly troubled by them, wondering why this power was bestowed upon him, and fearing lest it should make him less humble. This was not the frame of mind, nor was St. Bernard's the character, of a deluded enthusiast. The spiritualist need not believe that all this never happened; or that St. Francis d'Assisi and St. Theresa were not raised into the air, as eye-witnesses declared they were.

5. Witchcraft and witchcraft trials have a new interest for the spiritualist. He is able to detect hundreds of curious and minute coincidences with phenomena he has himself witnessed; he is able to separate the *facts* from the absurd *inferences*, which people imbued with the frightful superstition of diabolism drew from them, and from which false inferences all the horrors of the witchcraft mania arose. Spiritualism, and Spiritualism alone, gives a rational explanation of witchcraft, and determines how much of it was objective fact, how much subjective illusion.

6. Modern Roman Catholic miracles become intelligible facts. Spirits whose affections and passions are strongly excited in favour of Catholicism, produce those appearances of the Virgin and of saints which they know will tend to increased religious fervour. The appearance itself may be an objective reality; while it is only an inference that it is the Virgin Mary,--an inference which every intelligent spiritualist would repudiate as in the highest degree improbable.

7. Second-sight, and many of the so-called superstitions of savages, may be realities. It is well known that mediumistic power is more frequent and more energetic in mountainous countries; and as these are generally inhabited by the less civilised races, the beliefs that are more prevalent there may be due to the facts which are more prevalent, and be wrongly imputed to the coincident ignorance. It is known to spiritualists that the pure dry air of California led to more

powerful and more startling manifestations than in any other part of the United States.

8. The recently discussed question of the efficacy of prayer receives a perfect solution by Spiritualism. Prayer may be often answered, though not directly by the Deity. Nor does the answer depend wholly on the morality or the religion of the petitioner; but as men who are both moral and religious, and are firm believers in a divine response to prayer, will pray more frequently, more earnestly, and more disinterestedly, they will attract towards them a number of spiritual beings who sympathise with them, and who, when the necessary mediumistic power is present, will be able, as they are often willing, to answer the prayer. A striking case is that of George Müller, of Bristol, who has now for forty-four years depended wholly for his own support, and that of his wonderful charities, on answer to prayer. His "Narrative of Some of the Lord's Dealings with George Müller" (6th Ed. 1860), should have been referred to in the late discussion, since it furnishes a better demonstration that prayer is sometimes really answered than the hospital experiment proposed by Sir Henry Thomson could possibly have done. In this work we have a precise yearly statement of his receipts and expenditure for many years. He never asked any one or allowed any one to be asked, directly or indirectly, for a penny. No subscriptions or collections were ever made; yet from 1830 (when he married without any

income whatever) he has lived, brought up a family, and established institutions which have steadily increased, till now four thousand orphan children are educated and in part supported. It has happened hundreds of times, that there has been no food in his house and no money to buy any, or no food or milk or sugar for the children. Yet he never took a loaf or any other article on credit even for a day; and during the thirty years over which his narrative extends, neither he nor the hundreds of children dependent upon him for their daily food have ever been without a regular meal! They have lived, literally, from hand to mouth; and his one and only resource has been secret prayer. Here is a case which has been going on in the midst of us for forty years, and is still going on; it has been published to the world for many years, yet a warm discussion is carried on by eminent men as to the fact of whether prayer is or is not answered, and not one of them exhibits the least knowledge of this most pertinent and illustrative phenomenon! The spiritualist explains all this as a personal influence. The perfect simplicity, faith, boundless charity, and goodness of George Müller, have enlisted in his cause beings of a like nature; and his mediumistic powers have enabled them to work for him by influencing others to send him money, food, clothes, &c., all arriving, as we should say, just in the nick of time. The numerous letters he received with these gifts, describing the sudden and uncontrollable impulse the donors felt to send him a certain definite sum at a certain fixed time, such being the exact sum he was in want of, and had prayed for, strikingly illustrates the nature of the power at work. All this might be explained away, if it were partial and discontinuous; but when it continued to supply the daily wants of a life of unexampled charity, *for which no provision in advance was ever made* (for that Müller considered would show want of trust in God), no such explanation can cover the facts.

9. Spiritualism enables us to comprehend and find a place for, that long series of disturbances and occult phenomena of various kinds, which occurred previous to what are termed the modern Spiritual manifestations. Robert Dale Owen's works give a rather full account of this class of phenomena, which are most accurately recorded and philosophically treated by him. This is not the place to refer to them in detail; but one of them may be mentioned as showing how large an amount of unexplained mystery there was, even in our own country, before the world heard anything of modern Spiritualism. In 1841, Major Edward Moor, F.R.S., published a little book called "Bealings Bells," giving an account of mysterious bell-ringing in his house at Great Bealings, Suffolk, and which continued for fifty-three days. Every attempt to discover the cause, by himself, friends, and bell-hangers, were fruitless; and by no efforts, however violent, could the same clamorous and rapid ringing be produced. He wrote an account to the newspapers, requesting information bearing on the

subject, when, in addition to certain wise suggestions--of rats or a monkey as efficient causes--he received fourteen communications, all relating cases of mysterious bell-ringing in different parts of England, many of them lasting much longer than Major Moor's, and all remaining equally unexplained. One lasted eighteen months; another was in Greenwich Hospital, where neither clerk-of-the-works, bell-hanger, nor men of science could discover the cause. One clergyman wrote of disturbances of a most serious kind continued in his parsonage for *nine years*, and he was able to trace back their existence in the same house for *sixty years*. Another case had lasted *twenty years*, and could be traced back for a *century*. Some of the details of these cases are most instructive. Trick is absolutely the most incredible of all explanations. Spiritualism furnishes the explanation by means of analogous facts occurring every day, and forming part of the great system of phenomena which demonstrates the spiritual theory. Major Moor's book is very rare; but a good abstract of it is given in Owen's "Debateable Land," p -258.

Moral Teachings of Spiritualism.

We have now to explain the Theory of Human Nature, which is the outcome of the phenomena taken in their entirety, and is also more or less explicitly taught by the communications which purport to come from spirits. It may be briefly outlined as follows:--

1. Man is a duality, consisting of an organized spiritual form, evolved coincidently with and permeating the physical body, and having corresponding organs and development.

2. Death is the separation of this duality, and effects no change in the spirit, morally or intellectually.

3. Progressive evolution of the intellectual and moral nature is the destiny of individuals; the knowledge, attainments, and experience of earth-life forming the basis of spirit-life.

4. Spirits can communicate through properly-endowed mediums. They are attracted to those they love or sympathise with, and strive to warn, protect, and influence them for good, by mental impression when they cannot effect any more direct communication; but, as follows from clause (2), their communications will be fallible, and must be judged and tested just as we do those of our fellow-men.

The foregoing outline propositions will suggest a number of questions and difficulties, for the answers to which readers are referred to the works of R. D. Owen, Hudson Tuttle, Professor Hare, and the records of Spiritualism *passim*. Here I must pass on to explain with some amount of detail, how the theory leads to a pure system of morality with sanctions far more powerful and effective than any which either religious systems or philosophy have put forth.

This part of the subject cannot perhaps be better

introduced, than by referring to some remarks by Professor Huxley in a letter to the Committee of the Dialectical Society. He says,--"But supposing the phenomena to be genuine--they do not interest me. If anybody would endow me with the faculty of listening to the chatter of old women and curates at the nearest cathedral town, I should decline the privilege, having better things to do. And if the folk in the spiritual world do not talk more wisely and sensibly than their friends report them to do, I put them in the same category." This passage, written with the caustic satire in which the kind-hearted Professor occasionally indulges, can hardly mean, that if it were proved that men really continued to live after the death of the body, that fact would not interest him, merely because some of them talked twaddle? Many scientific men deny the spiritual source of the manifestations, on the ground that real, genuine spirits might reasonably be expected not to indulge in the common-place trivialities which do undoubtedly form the staple of ordinary spiritual communications. But surely Professor Huxley, as a naturalist and philosopher, would not admit this to be a reasonable expectation. Does he not hold the doctrine that there can be no effect, mental or physical, without an adequate cause; and that mental states, faculties, and idiosyncrasies, that are the result of gradual development and life-long--and even ancestral--habit, cannot be suddenly changed by any known or imaginable cause? And if (as the Professor would probably admit) a very large majority of those who daily depart this life are persons addicted to twaddle, persons who spend much of their time in low or trivial pursuits, persons whose pleasures are sensual rather than intellectual,--whence is to come the transforming power which is suddenly, at the mere throwing off the physical body, to change these into beings able to appreciate and delight in high and intellectual pursuits? The thing would be a miracle, the greatest of miracles, and surely Professor Huxley is the last man to contemplate innumerable miracles as part of the order of nature; and all for what? Merely *to save these people from the necessary consequences of their misspent lives.* For the essential teaching of Spiritualism is, that we are, all of us, in every act and thought, helping to build up a "mental fabric," which will be and constitute ourselves, more completely after the death of the body than it does now. Just as this fabric is well or ill built, so will our progress and happiness be aided or retarded. Just in proportion as we have developed our higher intellectual and moral nature, or starved it by disuse and by giving undue prominence to those faculties which secure us mere physical or selfish enjoyment, shall we be well or ill fitted for the new life we enter on. The noble teaching of Herbert Spencer, that men are best educated by being left to suffer the natural consequences of their actions, is the teaching of Spiritualism as regards the transition to another phase of life. There will be no imposed rewards or punishments; but every one will suffer the natural and inevitable consequences of a well or ill-spent life. The well-spent life is that in which those faculties which regard our personal physical well-being, are subordinated to those which regard our social and intellectual well-being, and the well-being of others; and that inherent feeling--which is so universal and so difficult to account for--that these latter constitute our higher nature, seems also to point to the conclusion that we are intended for a condition in which the former will be almost wholly unnecessary, and will gradually become rudimentary through disuse, while the latter will receive a corresponding development.

Although, therefore, the twaddle and triviality of so many of the communications is not one whit more interesting to sensible spiritualists than it is to Professor Huxley, and is never voluntarily listened to, yet the fact that such poor stuff is talked (supposing it to come from spirits) is both a fact that might have been anticipated and a lesson of deep import. We must remember, too, the character of the séances at which these common-place communications are received. A miscellaneous assemblance of believers of various grades and tastes, but mostly in search of an evening's amusement, and of sceptics who look upon all the others as either fools or knaves, is not likely to attract to itself the more elevated and refined denizens of the higher spheres, who may well be supposed to feel too much interest in their own new and grand intellectual existence to waste their energies on either class. If the fact is proved, that people continue to talk after they are dead with just as little sense as when alive, but that, being in a state in which sense, both common and uncommon, is of far greater importance to happiness than it is here (where fools pass very comfortable lives), they suffer the penalty of having neglected to cultivate their minds; and being so much out of their element in a world where all pleasures are mental, they endeavour to recall old times by gossiping with their former associates whenever they can find the means--Professor Huxley will not fail to see its vast importance as an incentive to that higher education which he is never weary of advocating. He would assuredly be interested in anything having a really practical bearing on the present as well as on the future condition of men; and it is evident that even these low and despised phenomena of Spiritualism, "if true," have this bearing, and, combined with its higher teachings, constitute a great moral agency which may yet regenerate the world.

For the spiritualist who, by daily experience, gets absolute knowledge of these facts regarding the future state--who knows that, just in proportion as he indulges in passion, or selfishness, or the exclusive pursuit of wealth, and neglects to cultivate the affections and the varied powers of his mind, so does he inevitably prepare for himself misery in a world in which there are no physical wants to be provided for, no sensual enjoyments except those directly associated with the affections and sympathies, no occupations but those having for their object social and intellectual progress--is impelled towards a pure, a sympathetic, and an intellectual life by motives far stronger than any which either religion or philosophy can supply. He dreads to give way to passion or to falsehood, to selfishness or to a life of luxurious physical enjoyment, because he knows that the natural and inevitable consequences of such habits are future misery, necessitating a long and arduous struggle in order to develope anew the faculties, whose exercise long disuse has rendered painful to him. He will be deterred from crime by the knowledge that its unforeseen consequences may cause him ages of remorse; while the bad passions which it encourages will be a perpetual torment to himself in a state of being in which mental emotions can not be laid aside or forgotten amid the fierce struggles and sensual pleasures of a physical existence. It must be remembered that these beliefs (unlike those of theology) will have a living efficacy, because they depend on *facts* occurring again and again in the family circle, constantly reiterating the same truths as the result of personal knowledge, and thus bringing home to the mind even of the most obtuse, the absolute reality of that future existence in which our degree of happiness or misery will be directly dependent on the "mental fabric" we construct by our daily thoughts, and words, and actions here.

Contrast this system of natural and inevitable reward

and retribution, dependent wholly on the proportionate development of our higher mental and moral nature, with the arbitrary system of rewards and punishments dependent on stated facts and beliefs only, as set forth by all dogmatic religions; and who can fail to see that the former is in harmony with the whole order of nature--the latter opposed to it. Yet it is actually said that Spiritualism is altogether either imposture or delusion, and all its teachings but the product of "expectant attention" and "unconscious cerebration"! If none of the long series of demonstrative facts which have been here sketched out, existed, and its only product were this theory of a future state, that alone would negative such a supposition. And when it is considered that mediums of all grades, whether intelligent or ignorant, and having communications given through them in various direct and indirect ways, are absolutely in accord as to the main features of this theory, what becomes of the gross misstatement that nothing is given through mediums but what they know and believe themselves? The mediums have, almost all, been brought up in some of the usual orthodox beliefs. How is it, then, that the usual orthodox notions of heaven are *never* confirmed through them? In the scores of volumes and pamphlets of spiritual literature I have read, I have found no statement of a spirit describing "winged angels," or "golden harps," or the "throne of God"--to which the humblest orthodox Christian thinks he will be introduced if he goes to heaven at all. There is no more startling and radical opposition to be found between the most diverse religious creeds, than that between the beliefs in which the majority of mediums have been brought up and the doctrines as to a future life that are delivered through them; there is nothing more marvellous in the history of the human mind than the fact that, whether in the back-woods of America or in country towns in England, ignorant men and women having almost all been brought up in the usual sectarian notions of heaven and hell, should, the moment they become seized by the strange power of mediumship, give forth teachings on this subject which are philosophical rather than religious, and which differ wholly from what had been so deeply ingrained into their minds. And this statement is not affected by the fact that communications purport to come from Catholic or Protestant, Mahomedan or Hindoo spirits. Because, while such communications maintain special *dogmas* and *doctrines*, yet they confirm the *very facts* which really constitute the spiritual theory, and which in themselves contradict the theory of the sectarian spirits. The Roman Catholic spirit, for instance, does not describe himself as being in either the orthodox purgatory, heaven, or hell; the Evangelical Dissenter who died in the firm conviction that he should certainly "go to Jesus," never describes himself as being with Christ, or as ever having seen Him, and so on throughout. Nothing is more common than for religious people at séances to ask questions about God and Christ. In reply they never get more than opinions, or more frequently the statement that they, the spirits, have no more actual knowledge of those subjects than they had while on earth. So that the facts are all harmonious; and the very circumstance of there being sectarian spirits bears witness in two ways to the truth of the spiritual theory--it shows that the mind, with its ingrained beliefs, is not suddenly changed at death; and it shows that the communications are not the reflection of the mind of the medium, who is often of the same religion as the communicating spirit, and, because he does not get his own ideas confirmed, is obliged to call in the aid of "Satanic influence" to account for the anomaly.

The doctrine of a future state and of the proper preparation for it as here developed, is to be found in the works of all spiritualists, in the utterances of all trance-speakers, in the communications through all mediums; and this could be proved, did space permit, by copious quotations. But it varies in form and detail in each; and just as the historian arrives at the opinions or beliefs of any age or nation, by collating the individual opinions of its best and most popular writers, so do spiritualists collate the various statements on this subject. They know well that absolute dependence is to be placed on no individual communications. They know that these are received by a complex physical and mental process, both communicator and recipient influencing the result; and they accept the teachings as to the future state of man only so far as they are repeatedly confirmed in substance (though they may differ in detail) by communications obtained under the most varied circumstances, through mediums of the most different characters and acquirements, at different times, and in different places. Fresh converts are apt to think, that, once satisfied the communications come from their deceased friends, they may implicitly trust to them, and apply them universally; as if the vast spiritual world was all moulded to one pattern, instead of being, as it almost certainly is, a thousand times more varied than human society on the earth is, or ever has been. The fact that the communications do not agree as to the condition, occupations, pleasures, and capacities, of individual spirits, so far from being a difficulty, as has been absurdly supposed, is what ought to have been expected; while the agreement on the essential features of what we have stated to be the spiritual theory of a future state of existence, is all the more striking, and tends to establish that theory as a fundamental truth.

The assertion, so often made, that Spiritualism is the survival or revival of old superstitions, is so utterly unfounded as to be hardly worth notice. A science of human nature which is founded on observed facts; which appeals only to facts and experiment; which takes no beliefs on trust; which inculcates investigation and self-reliance as the first duties of intelligent beings; which teaches that happiness in a future life can be secured by cultivating and developing to the utmost the higher faculties of our intellectual and moral nature *and by no other method,*--is and must be the natural enemy of all superstition. Spiritualism is an experimental science, and affords the only sure foundation for a true philosophy and a pure religion. It abolishes the terms "supernatural" and "miracle" by an extension of the sphere of law and the realm of nature; and in doing so it takes up and explains whatever is true in the superstitions and so-called miracles of all ages. It, and it alone, is able to harmonise conflicting creeds; and it must ultimately lead to concord among mankind in the matter of religion, which has for so many ages been the source of unceasing discord and incalculable evil;--and it will be able to do this because it appeals to evidence instead of faith, and substitutes facts for opinions; and is thus able to demonstrate the source of much of the teaching that men have so often held to be divine.

It will thus be seen, that those who can form no higher conception of the uses of Spiritualism, "even if true," than to detect crime or to name in advance the winner of the Derby, not only prove their own ignorance of the whole subject, but exhibit in a marked degree that partial mental paralysis, the result of a century of materialistic thought, which renders so many men unable seriously to conceive the possibility of a natural continuation of human life after the death of the body. It will be seen also that Spiritualism is no mere "physiological" curiosity, no mere indication of some hitherto unknown "law of nature;" but that it is a science of vast extent, having the widest, the most important, and the most practical issues, and as such should enlist the sympathies alike of moralists, philosophers, and politicians, and of all who have at heart the improvement of society and the permanent elevation of human nature.

In concluding this necessarily imperfect though somewhat lengthy account of a subject about which so little is probably known to most of the readers of the Fortnightly Review, I would earnestly beg them not to satisfy themselves with a minute criticism of single facts, the evidence for which, in my brief survey, may be imperfect; but to weigh carefully the mass of evidence I have adduced, considering its wide range and various bearings. I would ask them to look rather at the results produced by the evidence than at the evidence itself as imperfectly stated by me; to consider the long roll of men of ability who, commencing the inquiry as sceptics left it as believers, and to give these men credit for not having overlooked, during years of patient inquiry, difficulties which at once occur to themselves. I would ask them to ponder well on the fact, that no earnest inquirer has ever come to a conclusion adverse to the reality of the phenomena; and that no spiritualist has ever yet given them up as false. I would ask them, finally, to dwell upon the long series of facts in human history that Spiritualism explains, and on the noble and satisfying theory of a future life that it unfolds. If they will do this, I feel confident that the result I have alone aimed at will be attained; which is, to remove the prejudices and misconceptions with which the whole subject has been surrounded, and to incite to unbiassed and persevering examination of the facts. For the cardinal maxim of Spiritualism is, that every one must find out the truth for himself. It makes no claim to be received on hearsay evidence; but, on the other hand, it demands that it be not rejected without patient, honest, and fearless inquiry.

SPIRITUALISM AND CONJURORS

(S271: 1877)

A short time since there was a note in *The Spiritualist* to the effect that Dr. Lynn was exhibiting "burlesques of spiritual phenomena at the Aquarium." From Dr. Lynn's antecedents it seemed probable that this should be so, but probabilities are not facts. From what a friend informed me I had my doubts, and I therefore visited the Aquarium a few days back, and, with four other gentlemen, went on the stage to take part in the *séance*. Your readers must be told that Dr. Lynn is not the performer, but a gentleman who is introduced as "a medium--a real medium;" and I must say I believe him to be one. We first sat at a table--a very common and undoubtedly genuine table, which I turned over and examined, and after about four minutes' sitting this table rose up full two feet from the floor, and floated horizontally round the stage twice, resisting my efforts to stop it. All our hands were *on* the table; it moved about rapidly but somewhat irregularly; and no wires or machinery had anything to do with it. To me the motion was exactly such as I have experienced, with a genuine medium, but more powerful. Then followed the cabinet *séance*, the "cabinet" being a baize curtain supported by four poles on a carpet-covered platform, raised about a foot above the stage, and having no connection with it. We examined it thoroughly, and it was absolutely above suspicion. The medium was tied, hands and feet, in the usual way in a chair, by two gentlemen, and almost all the phenomena which characterised the Davenports' performance were here reproduced, but with even *greater rapidity*. At the very same instant that the curtain was drawn, hands appeared over the top, and the moment they descended the curtain was drawn back, and we found the medium with feet and hands tied exactly as before. This was repeated in various ways half a dozen times. Then, for an instant, three figures appeared in the cabinet robed in white from head to foot, and the next instant they disappeared, the medium being found tied as before, with no possibility of concealing the white robes, to say nothing of the figures which were there. The medium's coat was also removed and afterwards put on again, his hands remaining tied, and one of the spectators who entered the cabinet had his coat-sleeves turned inside out, and the coat put on him again without his being able to give any account of how it was done.

Now, it seems to me that a very bad effect will be produced by telling the public that this is all imposture; for they will naturally say, "We see no difference between this performance and those which you tell us are real: if this is imposture, then all your alleged spiritual manifestations are imposture also." I trust that you, Mr. Editor, or some of your readers, who have had more experience of mediums than I have had, will visit the Aquarium theatre and tell us your impressions after going on the stage; and if you think it is all juggling, point out exactly where the difference lies between it and mediumistic phenomena. I must also add, that when I was there Dr. Lynn said nothing against Spiritualists or Spiritualism. Of course, he made his usual fun, and referred to the risk of prosecution if he *said* it was all done by spirits--a remark which his audience took as an excellent joke, but which might have another meaning.

There have been many cases in which genuine clairvoyance has been brought before the public as conjuring; and now that the exhibition of anything claimed to be spiritual manifestations is punished by the strong arm of the law, it is to be expected that some physical mediums will engage themselves to professors of legerdemain in order to secure peace and safety. If the phenomena I have described are produced by conjuring, it is clear that Dr. Lynn, who is a master of the art, could do it himself and thereby add to his reputation; but he does not, and, as I venture to think, *cannot* do so, and until some one up to the tricks of conjurors really shows "how it is done," I shall continue to hold the opinion that we have here a case of genuine mediumship.

London, August 10th, 1877.

PSYCHOLOGICAL CURIOSITIES OF SCEPTICISM.
A REPLY TO DR. CARPENTER.

(S283: 1877)

In the last number of this periodical, Dr. Carpenter has treated his readers to a collection of what he terms 'Psychological Curiosities of Spiritualism.' Throughout his article he takes Mr. Crookes and myself as typical examples of men suffering under 'an Epidemic Delusion comparable to the Witchcraft Epidemic of the seventeenth century,' and he holds up our names to wonder and scorn because, after many years of inquiry, observation, and experiment, and after duly weighing all the doubts suggested and explanations proposed by Dr. Carpenter and others, we persist in accepting the uniform and consistent testimony of our senses. Are we indeed 'Psychological Curiosities' because we rely upon what philosophers assure us is our sole and ultimate test of truth--perception and reason? And should we be less rare and 'curious' phenomena if, rejecting as worthless all our personally acquired knowledge, we should blindly accept Dr. Carpenter's suggestions of what he *thinks* must have happened in place of what we *know* did happen? If such is the judgment of the world, we must for a time submit to the scorn and ridicule which usually fall to the lot of unpopular minorities, but we look forward with confidence to the advent of a higher class of critics than our present antagonist, critics who will not condescend to a style of controversy so devoid of good taste and impartiality as that adopted by Dr. Carpenter.

It is with great reluctance that I continue a discussion so purely personal as this has become, but I have really no choice. If Dr. Carpenter had contented himself with impugning my sanity or my sense on general grounds, I should not think it worth while to write a word in reply. But when I find my facts distorted and my words perverted, I feel bound to defend myself, not for the sake of my personal character, but in order to put a stop to a mode of discussion which renders all evidence unavailing and sets up unfounded and depreciatory assertions in the place of fair argument.

I now ask my readers to allow me to put before them the other side of this question, and I assure them that if they will read through this article they will acknowledge that the strong language I have used is fully justified by the facts which I shall adduce.

Those who believe in the reality of the abnormal

phenomena whose existence is denied by Dr. Carpenter and his followers, have, for the most part, been convinced by what they have seen in private houses and among friends on whose character they can rely. They constitute a not uninfluential body of literary and scientific men, including several Fellows of the Royal Society. The cases of public imposture (real or imaginary) so persistently adduced by Dr. Carpenter, do not affect their belief, which is altogether independent of public exhibitions; and they probably with myself look upon the learned Doctor (who tilts against facts as Don Quixote did against windmills, and with equally prejudicial results to himself) as a curious example of fossilised scepticism. Thus, Serjeant Cox, who often quotes Dr. Carpenter and is now quoted by him with approval, speaks of the learned Doctor (in his recent address to the Psychological Society) as being 'enslaved and blinded' by 'prepossession,' adding:

There is not a more notable instance of this than Dr. Carpenter himself, whose emphatic warnings to beware of it are doubtless the result of self-consciousness. An apter illustration of this human weakness there could not be. The characteristic feature of his mind is prepossession. This weakness is apparent in all his works. It matters not what the subject, if once he has formed an opinion upon it, that opinion so prepossesses his whole mind that nothing adverse to it can find admission there. It affects alike his senses and his judgment.

I propose, therefore, as a companion picture to that of Messrs. Crookes and Wallace the victims of an Epidemic Delusion, to exhibit Dr. Carpenter as an example of what prepossession and blind scepticism can do for a man. I shall show how it makes a scientific man unscientific, a wise man foolish, an honest man unjust. To refuse belief to unsupported rumours of improbable events, is enlightened scepticism; to reject all second-hand or anonymous tales to the injury or depreciation of anyone, is charitable scepticism; to doubt your own prepossessions when opposed to facts observed and re-observed by honest and capable men, is a noble scepticism. But the scepticism of Dr. Carpenter is none of these. It is a blind, unreasoning, arrogant disbelief, that marches on from youth to age with its eyes shut to all that opposes its own pet theories; that believes its own judgment to be infallible; that never acknowledges its errors. It is a scepticism that clings to its refuted theories, and refuses to accept new truths.

Near the commencement of his article Dr. Carpenter tells us that he recurs to this subject as a duty to the public and to assist in curing a dangerous mental disease; and that he would gladly lay it aside for the scientific investigations which afford him the purest enjoyment. But he also tells us that he honestly believes that he possesses 'unusual power of dealing with this subject;' and as Dr. Carpenter is not one to hide the light of his 'unusual powers' under a bushel, we may infer that it is not pure duty which has caused him, in addition to writing long letters to *Nature* and announcing a 'full answer' to myself and Mr. Crookes in the forthcoming new edition of his Lectures, to expend his valuable time and energy on an article of forty-eight columns, founded mainly on such a very shaky and *un*-scientific foundation as American newspaper extracts and the unsupported statements of Mr. Home, the medium;[1] while it is full of personal animosity and the most unmeaning ridicule. With extreme bad taste he compares a gentleman, who, as a scholar, a thinker, and a writer, is Dr. Carpenter's equal, to Moses and Son's kept poet; while with a pitiable inappropriateness he parodies the fine though hackneyed saying, 'See how these Christians love one another,' in order to apply it satirically to the case of a rather severe, but not unfair, review of Mr. Home's book in a Spiritual periodical.

I will now proceed to show, not only that my accusations in the *Quarterly Journal of Science* for July last--which in Dr. Carpenter's opinion amount to a charge of 'wilful and repeated *suppressio veri*'--are proved, but that a blind reliance on Mr. Home and on 'excerpts from American newspapers' have led him to make deliberate statements which are totally unfounded.

I will first take a case which will illustrate Dr. Carpenter's wonderful power of mis-statement as regards myself.

1. In a letter to the *Daily News* written immediately after

the delivery of Dr. Carpenter's first Lecture on Mesmerism at the London Institution a year ago, I adduced a case of mesmerism at a distance recorded by the late Professor Gregory. The lady mesmerised was a relation of the Professor and was staying in his own house. The mesmeriser was a Mr. Lewis. The sole authority for the facts referred to by me was *Professor Gregory himself.*

2. While criticising this Mr. Lewis in his Lectures (page 24) Dr. Carpenter says, referring to my *Daily News* letter, 'His (Mr. Lewis's) utter failure to produce either result, however, under the scrutiny of sceptical inquirers, obviously discredits all *his previous statements*; except to such as (like Mr. A. R. Wallace, who has recently *expressed his full faith in Mr. Lewis's self-asserted powers*) are ready to accept without question the slenderest evidence of the greatest marvels.' (The italics are my own.)

3. In my 'Review' of Dr. Carpenter's book (*Quarterly Journal of Science*, July 1877, page 394) I use strong (but, I submit, appropriate) language as to this injurious and unfounded statement. For Dr. Carpenter's readers must have understood, and must have been intended to understand, that, in sole reliance on this Mr. Lewis's *own statements*, I placed full faith in them without any corroboration, and had also publicly announced this faith; in which case his readers would have been justified in thinking me a credulous fool not worth listening to.

4. Writing again on this subject (in last month's issue of this Magazine,) Dr. Carpenter does not apologise for the gross and injurious misrepresentation of what I really said, neither does he justify it by reference to anything else I may have written; but he covers his retreat with a fresh *suggestio jalsi*, and ridicules me for using such strong language (which he quotes) merely (he says) because he had reflected on my 'too ready acceptance of the slenderest evidence of the greatest marvels'--a phrase of Dr. Carpenter's which I never objected to at all because it was a mere expression of opinion, while what I did object to was a mis-statement of a matter of fact. This is Dr. Carpenter's idea of the way to carry on that 'calm discussion with other men of science' to the absence of which he imputes all my errors. (Note A, .)

Dr. Carpenter is so prepossessed with the dominant idea of putting down Spiritualism, that it seems impossible for him to state the simplest fact in regard to it without introducing some purely imaginary fact of his own to make it fit his theory. Thus, in his article on 'The Fallacies of Testimony' (*Contemporary Review*, 1876,) he says: 'A whole party of believers will affirm that they saw Mr. Home float out of one window and in at another, whilst a single honest sceptic *declares* that Mr. Home was sitting in his chair *all the time*.' Now there is only one case on record of Mr. Home having 'floated out of one window and in at another.' Two of the persons present on the occasion--Lord Adare and Lord

Lindsay--have made public their account of it, and the third has never declared that Mr. Home was 'sitting in his chair all the time,' but has privately confirmed, to the extent his position enabled him to do so, the testimony of the other two. Is this another case of Dr. Carpenter 'cerebrating' his facts to suit his theory, or will he say it is a purely hypothetical case? Yet this can hardly be, for he goes on to argue from it: 'And in this last case we have an example of a *fact*, of which &c. &c.' I ask Dr. Carpenter to name the 'honest sceptic' of this quotation and to give us his precise statement; or, failing this, to acknowledge that he has imagined a piece of evidence to suit his hypothesis. (Note B, .)

It is only fair that he should do this because, in another of his numerous raids upon the poor deluded spiritualists, he has made a direct and, as it seems to me, completely unsupported charge against Lord Lindsay. In his article on 'Spiritualism and its recent Converts' (*Quarterly Review*, 1871, p , 336) Dr. Carpenter quotes Lord Lindsay's account of an experiment with Mr. Home, in which Lord Lindsay placed a powerful magnet in one corner of a totally dark room, and then brought in the medium, who after a few moments said he saw a sort of light on the floor; and to prove it led Lord Lindsay straight to the spot and placed his hand upon the magnet. The experiment was not very remarkable, but still, so far as it went, it confirmed the observations of Reichenbach and others. This Dr. Carpenter cannot bear; so he not only proceeds to point out Lord Lindsay's complete ignorance of the whole subject but makes him morally culpable for not having used Dr. Carpenter's pet test of an electro-magnet; and he concludes thus: 'If, then, Lord Lindsay cannot be trusted as a "faithful" witness in "that which is least," how can we feel assured that he is "faithful also in much"?' By what mental jugglery Dr. Carpenter can have convinced himself that he had shown that Lord Lindsay 'cannot be trusted as a faithful witness,' I am at a loss to understand. But the *animus* against the friend of and believer in Mr. Home, is palpable. Now that Lord Lindsay has achieved a scientific reputation, we presume there must be two Lord Lindsays as well as two Mr. Crookes': one the enthusiastic astronomer and careful observer, the other the deluded spiritualist and 'psychological curiosity.' As these double people increase it will become rather puzzling, and we shall have to adopt Mr. Crookes' prefixes of 'Ortho' and 'Pseudo' to know which we are talking about.[2] It will be well also to note the Scriptural language employed by Dr. Carpenter in making this solemn and ridiculously unfounded charge. It reminds one of the 'I speak advisedly' (in the celebrated *Quarterly Review* article now acknowledged by Dr. Carpenter) which Mr. Crookes has shown to be in every case the prefix of a wholly incorrect statement.[3]

Dr. Carpenter heads a section of his article in last month's issue of this periodical, 'What Mr. Wallace means by Demonstration;' and endeavours to show that I have misapplied the term when I stated that in certain cases flowers had appeared at *séances* 'demonstrably not brought by the medium.' His long quotations from Mr. Home, giving purely imaginary and burlesque accounts of such *séances*, totally unauthenticated by names or dates, may be set aside as not only irrelevant but as insulting to the readers who are asked to accept them as evidence. Dr. Carpenter begins by confounding the proof of a *fact* and that of a *proposition*, and, against the view of the best modern philosophers, maintains that the latter alone can be truly said to be 'demonstrated.' But this is a complete fallacy. The direct testimony of the educated senses guided by reason, is of higher validity than any complex result of reason alone. If I am sitting with two friends and a servant brings me a letter, I am justified in saying that that letter was 'demonstrably not brought by one of my friends.' Or if a bullet comes through the window and strikes the wall behind me, I am justified in saying that one of my two friends sitting at the table 'demonstrably did not fire the pistol;'--always supposing that I am proved to be in the full possession of my ordinary senses by the general agreement of my friends with me as to what happened. Of course if I am in a state of delusion or insanity, and my senses and reasoning powers do not record events in agreement with others who witness them, neither shall I be able to perceive the force of a mathematical demonstration. If my senses play me false, squares may seem to me triangles and circles ellipses, and no geometrical reasoning will be possible. Dr. Carpenter next asserts that I 'complain' of his 'not accepting the flowers and fruits produced in my own drawing-room and those which made their appearance in the house of Mr. T. A. Trollope at Florence.' This is simply not the case. I never asked him to accept them or complained of his not accepting them; but I pointed out that he did accept the evidence of a prejudiced witness to support a theory of imposture which was entirely negatived in the two cases I referred to.[4] I implied, that he should either leave the subject alone or deal with the *best* evidence of the alleged facts. To do otherwise was not 'scientific,' and to put anonymous and unsupported evidence before the public as conclusive of the whole question was both unscientific and disingenuous. Now that he does attempt to deal with these cases, he makes them explicable on his own theory of imposture only by leaving out the most essential facts.

He first says that 'in Mr. Wallace's own case no precautions whatever had been employed!' and he introduces this with the remark, 'Now it will scarcely be believed,' to which I will add that it must not be believed, because it is untrue. I have never published a *detailed* account of this *séance*, but I have stated the main facts with sufficient care[5] to show that the phenomenon itself was a test surpassing anything that could have been prearranged. The general precautions used by me were as follows: Five personal friends were present besides myself and the medium, among them a medical man, a barrister, and an acute colonial man of business. The sitting was in my own back drawing-room. No cloth was on the table. The adjoining room and passage were fully lighted. We sat an hour in the darkened room before the flowers appeared, but there was always light enough to see the outlines of those present. We sat a little away from the table, the medium sitting by me. The flowers appeared on the polished table dimly visible as a *something*, before we lighted the gas. When we did so the whole surface of the four-feet circular table was covered with fresh flowers and ferns, a sight so beautiful and marvellous, that in the course of a not uneventful life I can hardly recall anything that has more strongly impressed me. I begged that nothing might be touched till we had carefully examined them. The first thing that struck us all was their extreme freshness and beauty. The next, that they were all covered, especially the ferns, with a delicate dew; not with coarse drops of water as I have since seen when the phenomenon was less perfect, but with a veritable fine dew, covering the whole surface of the ferns especially. Counting the separate sprigs we found them to be forty-eight in number, consisting of four yellow and red tulips, eight large anemones of various colours, six large flowers of *Primula japonica*, eighteen chrysanthemums mostly yellow and white, six fronds of Lomaria a foot long, and two of a Nephrodium about a foot long and six inches wide. Not a pinnule of these ferns was rumpled, but they lay on the table as perfect as if freshly brought from a conservatory. The anemones, primroses, and tulips had none of them lost a petal. They were found spread over the whole surface of the table, while we had been for some time intently gazing on the sheen of its surface and could have instantly detected a hand and arm moving over it. But that is not so important as the *condition* of these flowers and their dewiness; and-- Dr. Carpenter notwithstanding--I still maintain they were (to us) 'demonstrably not brought by the medium.' I have preserved the flowers and have them now before me, with the attestation of all present as to their appearance and condition; and I have also my original notes made at the time. How simple is Dr. Carpenter's notion that I tell this story, after ten years, from memory! How ingenious is his suggestion of the *lining of a cloak* as their place of concealment for four hours--a suggestion taken from a second-hand story by Mr. Home about a paid medium, and therefore *not* the lady whose powers are now under discussion! How utterly beside the question his subsequent remarks about conjurors, and hats, and the mango-trees produced by Indian jugglers!

In the case certified by Mr. T. A. Trollope the medium's person (not her dress only, as Dr. Carpenter says) was carefully searched before sitting down; but now it is objected that 'an experienced female searcher' would have been more satisfactory, and the fact is ignored that phenomena occurred which precluded the necessity of any search. For while the medium's hands were both held a large quantity of jonquils fell on the table, 'filling the whole room with their odour.' If Dr. Carpenter can get over the 'sudden falling on the table' of the flowers while the medium's hands were held, how does he explain the withholding of the powerful odour 'filling the whole room' till the moment of their appearance? Mr. Trollope says that this is, 'on any common theory of physics, unaccountable,' and I say that this large quantity of powerfully smelling jonquils was 'demonstrably not brought by the medium.' I have notes of other cases equally well attested. In one of these at a friend's house to which I myself took Miss Nicholl, eighty separate stalks of flowers and ferns fell on the table while the medium's hands were both held. All were perfectly fresh and damp, and some large sprays of maiden-hair fern were quite perfect. On another occasion I was present when twenty different kinds of fruits were asked for, and every person had their chosen kind placed before them on the table or put at once into their hands by some invisible agency. These cases might be multiplied indefinitely, and many are recorded which are still more completely beyond the power of imposture to explain. But all such are passed over by Dr. Carpenter in silence. He asks for better evidence of certain facts, and when we adduce it he says we are the victims of a 'diluted insanity.'[6] In the supposed Belfast exposure by means of potassium ferrocyanide, I objected that the only evidence was that of a prejudiced witness with a strong *animus* against the medium. Dr. Carpenter now prints this young man's letter (of which he had in his lecture given the substance) and thinks that he has transformed his *one* witness into *two* by means of an anonymous 'friend' therein mentioned. He talks of the 'immediate detection of the salt by *one* witness and the subsequent confirmatory testimony of the *other*'-- this 'other' being the anonymous friend of the 'one witness' letter! Unfortunately this 'friend' wrote a letter to the papers in which he brought an additional accusation, which I have proved, by the testimony of an unimpeachable witness, to be utterly unfounded. (See *Quarterly Journal of Science*, July 1877, .) We may therefore dismiss the 'exposure' as, to say the least, not proven.

Dr. Carpenter heads one of his sections, 'What Messrs. Wallace and Crookes regard as "Trustworthy Testimony";' and before I remark on its contents, I wish to point out the literary impropriety of which Dr. Carpenter is guilty, in thus making Mr. Crookes responsible for the whole contents of my article in the *Quarterly Journal of Science* because he happens to be the editor of that periodical. I might with equal justice charge upon the editor of *Fraser* all the mis-statements and injurious personal imputations which Dr. Carpenter has introduced into an article, accepted, doubtless, without question on the strength of his high scientific standing.

Under the above heading Dr. Carpenter attempts to show that Colonel Olcott (whose investigation into the character of Mrs. White and her false declaration that she had, on certain occasions, personated 'Katie King,' I quoted in my review) is an untrustworthy witness; and his sole proof consists in a quotation from a published letter of the Colonel's about bringing an 'African sorcerer' to America. This letter may or may not be injudicious or foolish; that is matter of opinion. But how it in any way 'blackens' Colonel Olcott's character or proves him to be 'untrustworthy' as a witness to matters of fact, it must puzzle everyone but a Carpenter or a Home to understand.

The next example I shall give of Dr. Carpenter's 'unusual power of dealing with this subject,' is a most injurious misstatement referring to my friend Mr. Crookes. Dr. Carpenter heads a section of more than eight columns, 'Mr. Crookes and his Scientific Tests,' and devotes it to an account of Eva Fay's performances, of Mr. Crookes' 'inconsiderate endorsement of one of the grossest impostures ever practised,' and of the alleged exposure of the fraud by Mr. W. Irvine Bishop. The following quotation contains the essence of the charge, and I invite particular attention to its wording:

. . . her London audiences diminishing away, Eva Fay returned to the United States, carrying with her a letter from Mr. Crookes, which set forth that since doubts had been thrown on the spiritualistic nature of her 'manifestations,' and since he, in common with other Fellows of the Royal Society, had satisfied themselves of their genuineness by 'scientific tests,' he willingly gave her the benefit of his attestation. This letter was published in *fac-simile* in American newspapers.

I can scarcely expect my readers at once to credit what I now have to state; that, notwithstanding the above precise setting forth of its contents, by a man who professes to write under a sense of duty, and as one called upon to rehabilitate the injured dignity of British Science, such a letter as that above minutely described never existed at all! A private letter from Mr. Crookes has indeed, without his consent, been published in *fac-simile* in American newspapers; but this letter was *never* in the possession of Eva Fay; it was not written till months after she had left England, and then not to her, but in answer to inquiries by a perfect stranger; moreover it contains not a word in any way resembling the passages above given! Sad to say, Dr. Carpenter's kind Boston friends do not appear to have sent him a copy of the paper containing the *fac-simile* letter, or he would have seen that Mr. Crookes says *nothing* of 'the spiritualistic nature of her manifestations;' he does *not* mention 'other Fellows of the Royal Society;' he does *not* say he was 'satisfied of the genuineness of the scientific tests,' but especially guards himself by saying that the published account of the experiments made at his own house are the best evidence of his belief in her powers. He does *not* 'give her the benefit of his attestation,' but simply says that no one has any authority to use his name to injure her.

The number of the *New York Daily Graphic* for April 12, 1876, containing the letter in *fac-simile* is now before me. An exact copy of it is given below, and I ask my readers to peruse it carefully, to compare it with Dr. Carpenter's precise summary given *as if from actual inspection*, and then decide by whose instrumentality the honoured distinction of F.R.S. is being 'trailed through the dirt,' and who best upholds his own reputation and that of British Science. Is it the man who writes a straightforward letter in order to prevent his name being used to injure another, and who states only facts within his own personal knowledge; or is it he who, for the express purpose of depreciating the well-earned reputation of a fellow man of science, publishes without a word of caution or hesitation a purely imaginary account of it?

MR. CROOKES' 'FAC-SIMILE' LETTER.

Nov. 8, 1875.
To R. Cooper, Esq.
c/o C. Maynard, Esq.
223 Washington Street,
Boston, Mass. U.S.A.

Dear Sir,

In reply to your avour of Oct. 25, which I have received this morning, I beg to state that no one has any authority from me to state that I have any doubts of Mrs. Fay's mediumship. The published accounts of the test *séances* which took place at my house are the best evidence which I can give of my belief in Mrs. Fay's powers. I should be sorry to find that any such rumours as you mention should injure Mrs. Fay, whom I have always found most ready to submit to any conditions I thought fit to propose. Believe me, very truly yours,

William Crookes.

Notwithstanding this attack, all the evidence Dr. Carpenter can adduce as to the alleged exposure of Eva Fay has really no bearing whatever on Mr. Crookes' position. Long and wordy letters are given *verbatim* which only amount to this: that the writers saw a clever conjuror do what they *thought* was an exact imitation of Eva Fay's performances and of those of mediums generally. But a most essential point is omitted. Neither of the three writers say *they ever saw Eva Fay's performance*. Still less do they say they ever saw her *in private* and *tested her themselves*; and without this their evidence is absolutely worthless. Mr. Crookes has said nothing, good or bad, about her public performances; but she came *alone* to his own house, and there, aided by scientific friends, in his own laboratory, he tested her by placing her in an electrical circuit from which she could not possibly escape or even attempt to escape without instant discovery. Yet when in this position books were taken from the bookcase twelve feet away and handed out to the observers. The beautiful arrangements by which these tests were carried out are detailed by Mr. Crookes in the *Spiritualist* newspaper of March 12, 1875, and should be read by everyone who wishes to understand the real difference between the methods of procedure of Mr. Crookes and Dr. Carpenter. Not one word is said, either by Dr. Carpenter's correspondents or by the *Daily Graphic*, as to *this* test having been applied to Mr. Bishop by an electrical engineer or other expert, and till this is done how can Mr. Crookes' position be in any way affected? A public performance in Boston, parodying that of Miss Fay, but without one particle of proof that the conditions of the two performances were really identical,[8] is to Dr. Carpenter's logical and sceptical mind a satisfactory proof that one of the first experimenters of the day was imposed on in his own laboratory, when assisted by trained experts, and when applying the most absolute tests that science can supply.[2] (Note C, .)

I have now shown to the readers of *Fraser* (as I had previously shown in the *Quarterly Journal of Science*) that whatever Dr. Carpenter writes on this subject, whether opinion, argument, quotation, or fact, is so distorted by prejudice as to be untrustworthy. It is therefore unnecessary here to reply in detail to the mass of innuendo and assumption that everywhere pervades his article; neither am I called upon to notice all the alleged 'exposures' which he delights in placing before his readers. To 'expose' malingerers and cases of feigned illness does not disprove the existence of disease; and if, as I believe has been demonstrated, the phenomena here discussed are marvellous realities, it is to be expected that there will be impostors to imitate them, and no lack of credulous persons to be duped by those impostors. But it is not the part of an honest searcher after truth to put forward these detected impostures while ignoring the actual phenomena which the impostors try to imitate. When we have Dr. Carpenter's final word in the promised new edition of his Lectures, I shall be prepared to show that tests far more severe than such as have resulted in the detection of imposture have been over and over again applied to the genuine phenomena with no other result than to confirm their genuineness.

This is not the place to discuss the reality of the phenomena which Dr. Carpenter rejects with so much misplaced indignation, and endeavours to put down by such questionable means. The careful observations of such men as Professor Barrett of Dublin, and the elaborate series of test experiments carried out in his own laboratory by Mr. Crookes,[10] are sufficient to satisfy any unprejudiced person that the phenomena are genuine; and if so, whatever theory we may adopt concerning them, they must greatly influence all our fundamental ideas in science and philosophy. The attempt to excite prejudice against all who have become convinced that these things are real, by vague accusations, and by quoting all the trash that can be picked out of the literature of the subject, is utterly unworthy of the men of science who adopt it. For nearly thirty years this plan has been unsparingly pursued, and its failure has been complete. Belief in the genuineness of the phenomena has grown steadily year by year; and at this day there are, to my personal knowledge, a larger number of well-educated and intelligent and even of scientific men who profess their belief, than at any former period. There is no greater mistake than to suppose that this body of inquirers have obtained their present convictions by what they have seen at public *séances* only. In almost every case those convictions are the result of a long series of experiments in private houses; and it would amaze Dr. Carpenter to learn the number of families in every class of society in which even the more marvellous and indisputable of these phenomena occur. The course taken by Dr. Carpenter of discrediting evidence, depreciating character, and retailing scandal, only confirms these people in their belief that men of science are powerless in face of this great subject; and I feel sure that all he has written has never converted a single earnest investigator.

It is well worthy of notice, as correlating this inquiry with other branches of science, that there is no royal road to acquiring a competent knowledge of these phenomena, and this is the reason why so many scientific men fail to obtain evidence of anything important. They think that a few hours should enable them to decide the whole thing; as if a problem which has been ever before the world, and which for the last quarter of a century has attracted the attention of thousands, only required their piercing glance to probe it to the bottom. But those who have devoted most time and study to the subject, though they become ever more convinced of the reality, the importance, and the endless phases of the phenomena, find themselves less able to dogmatise as to their exact nature or theoretical interpretation. Of one thing, however, they feel convinced; that all further discussion on the inner nature of man and his relation to the universe is a mere beating of the air so long as these marvellous phenomena, opening up as they do a whole world of new interactions between mind and matter, are disregarded and ignored.

APPENDIX.

Abstract of Mr. Crookes' Experiments above referred to.

The apparatus used consisted of an electrical circuit with a reflecting galvanometer showing the slightest variations in the current, designed and arranged by one of the most eminent practical electricians. This instrument was fixed in Mr. Crookes' laboratory, from which two stout wires passed through the wall into the library adjoining, and there terminated in two brass handles fixed at a considerable distance apart, and having only an inch or two of play. These handles are covered with linen soaked in salt and water, and when the person to be experimented on holds these handles in the hands (also first soaked in salt and water) the current of electricity passes through his or her body, and the exact 'electrical resistance' can be measured; while the reflecting galvanometer renders visible to all the spectators the slightest variation in the resistance. This instrument is so delicate that the mere loosening of the grasp of one or both hands or the lifting of a finger from the handle would be shown at once, because by altering the amount of surface in contact the 'electrical resistance' would be instantly changed. Two experienced physicists, both Fellows of the Royal Society, made experiments with this instrument for more than an hour before the tests began, and satisfied themselves that, even with an exact knowledge of what was required and with any amount of preparation, they could not substitute anything connecting the two handles and having the same exact resistance as the human body without a long course of trial and failure, and without a person in the other room to tell them if more or less resistance were required, during which time the index spot of light of the galvanometer was flying wildly about. Comparative steadiness of the index could only be secured by a steady and continuous grasp of the two handles.

Having thus described the apparatus, let us now consider how the test was carried out. The gentlemen invited to witness it were three Fellows of the Royal Society, all of special eminence, and three other gentlemen. They examined the library; fastened up the door to the passage as well as the window with strips of paper sealed with their private seals; they examined all the cupboards and desks; they noted the position of various articles, and measured their distances as well as that of the bookcase from the handles to be held by the medium. The library was connected with the laboratory by a door close to where the medium sat, and this door was wide open, but the aperture was closed by means of a curtain. Everything having been thus arranged, Eva Fay was invited to enter the library, having up to this time been in the drawing-room upstairs, and having come to the house *alone*. She then seated herself in a chair placed for the purpose, and having moistened her hands as directed took hold of the two handles. The exact 'electrical resistance' of her body was then noted, as well as the deflection shown by the galvanometer: and the gas in the library having been turned down low, the gentlemen took their places in the laboratory, leaving Eva Fay alone.

In one minute a hand-bell was rung in the library. In two minutes a hand came out at the side of the door farthest from the medium. During the succeeding five minutes four separate books were handed out to their respective authors, a voice from the library calling them by name. These books had been taken from the bookcase twelve feet from Eva Fay: they had been found in the dark, and one of them had no lettering on the back. Mr. Crookes declares that although he, of course, knew the general position of the books in his own library, he could not have found these books in the dark. Then a box of cigars was thrown out to a gentleman very fond of smoking, and finally an ornamental clock which had been standing on the chimney-piece was handed out. Then the circuit was suddenly broken, and on instantly entering the library Eva Fay was found lying back in the chair senseless, a condition in which she remained for half an hour. All the above phenomena occurred during the space of ten minutes, and the reflecting galvanometer was steady the whole time, showing only those small variations which would occur while a person continued to hold the handles.

On two other occasions Mr. Crookes carried out similar

tests with the same medium and always with the same result. On one occasion several musical instruments were played on at the same time and a musical box was wound up while the luminous index of the galvanometer continued quite steady, and many articles were handed or thrown out into the laboratory. On the other occasion similar things happened, after all possible precautions had been taken; and in addition Mr. Crookes' desk, which was carefully locked before the *séance*, was found unlocked and open at its conclusion.

Everyone must look forward with great interest to Dr. Carpenter's promised 'explanation' of how all these scientific tests were evaded by an unscientific impostor.

NOTE A.--Since this article was in the printer's hands a proof-sheet of the new edition of Dr. Carpenter's Lectures has been forwarded to me at the author's request, in order that I may see what further explanations he has to give of the above case. Dr. Carpenter now attempts to justify his assertion that I had 'recently *expressed* my full faith in Mr. Lewis' *self-asserted powers*,' by a statement of what Dr. Simpson told him several years ago, a statement which appears to have been never yet made public, and which, therefore, could not possibly have been taken into account by me, even had it any real bearing on the question at issue. It is to the effect that Mr. Lewis *might* have received information of the exact hour at which the lady he had promised to try to mesmerise at a distance, fell asleep in Professor Gregory's house, and that he *might* have afterwards given a false statement of the hour at which he attempted to mesmerise her. Dr. Carpenter is excessively indignant when any doubt is thrown by me on the truthfulness or impartiality of any of his informants, but it seems the most natural thing in the world for him to charge falsehood or fraud against all who testify to facts which he thinks incredible. But even admitting that Dr. Carpenter's memory of what was told him many years ago is absolutely perfect, and admitting that Mr. Lewis (against whose moral character nothing whatever is adduced) would have told a direct falsehood in order to magnify his own powers, how does this account for the fact that the lady was overcome by the mesmeric sleep at all, when her mind and body were both actively engaged at the piano early in the afternoon? And how does it account for the headache which had troubled her the whole day suddenly ceasing? It is not attempted to be shown that Mr. Lewis' statement--that he returned home at the hour named and at once proceeded to try and mesmerise the lady--is not true; so that, except for the supposed incredibility of the whole thing in Dr. Carpenter's opinion, there would be no reason to doubt the exact correctness of the statements made. But even if the reader adopts the view that Mr. Lewis was really an impostor, that does not make Dr. Carpenter's original assertion--that

I had 'expressed' my full faith in his 'self-asserted powers'--one whit more accurate. If Dr. Carpenter had then in his memory this means of throwing doubt on the facts, why did he not mention it in his Lectures or in his article, instead of first charging me with the 'expression' of a faith which I never expressed or held, and then attempting to change the issue by substituting other words for those which I really complained of?

NOTE B.--In the new edition of Dr. Carpenter's Lectures (the proof of part of which has been sent me) he supports his statement that--'there are at the present time numbers of educated men and women who have so completely surrendered their "common sense" to a dominant prepossession, as to maintain that any such monstrous fiction (as of a person being carried through the air in an hour from Edinburgh to London) ought to be believed, even upon the evidence of a single witness, if that witness be one upon whose testimony we should rely in the ordinary affairs of life,'--by saying that--'the moonlight sail of Mr. Home is extensively believed on the testimony of a single witness.' Even if it were the fact that this particular thing is believed by some persons on the testimony of a single witness, that would not justify Dr. Carpenter's statement that there are numbers of educated men and women who maintain as a principle that any such thing, however monstrous, *ought* to be so believed. As, however, there are, as above shown, *three* witnesses in this case, and at least *ten* in the case of Mrs. Guppy, also referred to, it appears that Dr. Carpenter first makes depreciatory general statements, and when these are challenged, supports them by a mis-statement of facts. Such a course of procedure renders further discussion impossible.

NOTE C.--A letter of Dr. Carpenter's has also 'at his own request' been forwarded to me, in which he attempts to justify the conduct narrated above. In *Nature* for November 15 Mr. Crookes printed the letter which was given in *fac-simile* in American newspapers, with remarks of a somewhat similar character to those I have here made. Dr. Carpenter, writing three days afterwards (November 18), wishes it to be stated in *Fraser* as his 'own correction,' that this letter was *not* carried away from England by Eva Fay; adding--'What was carried away by Eva Fay was *a much stronger attestation, publicly given in full detail by Mr. Crookes* in a communication to the *Spiritualist*;'--of which communication I give an abstract in an appendix to this article. This obliges me to add a few further particulars.

In *Nature*, October 25, in a note to a letter about the Radiometer, Dr. Carpenter says: "'On the strength of a private letter from Mr. Crookes, which has been published in *fac-simile* in the American newspapers, a certain Mrs. Or Miss Eva Fay announced her "spiritualistic" performances as endorsed by Prof. Crookes and other Fellows of the Royal Society.'" This supposed letter was 'set forth' in detail in last month's *Fraser* as above stated.

In *Nature*, November 8, Dr. Carpenter says, 'And the now notorious impostor, Eva Fay, has been able to appeal to the "endorsement" given to her by the "scientific tests" applied to her by "Professor Crookes and other Fellows of the Royal Society," which had been published (I now find) by Mr. Crookes himself in the *Spiritualist* in March, 1875.'

From the above it follows, that it was between October 25 and November 8 that Dr. Carpenter *first* became acquainted with Mr. Crookes' account of his experiments with Eva Fay; and finding (from Mr. Crookes' publication of it) that his own detailed account of the contents of the *fac-simile* letter was totally incorrect, he now makes a fresh assertion--that Eva Fay 'carried away with her' a copy of the *Spiritualist* containing Mr. Crookes' experiments. This is highly probable, but we venture to doubt if Dr. Carpenter has any authority to state it as a fact; while even if she did, that article does not, any more than the *fac-simile* letter, justify Dr. Carpenter's allegations. It contains not one word about the 'Spiritualistic nature of her manifestations,'--it does *not* state that he 'in common with other Fellows of the Royal Society had satisfied himself of their genuineness'--it does *not* say that he 'willingly gave her the benefit of his attestation.' It is a detailed account of a beautiful scientific experiment, and nothing more. Yet Dr. Carpenter still maintains (in his letter now before me) that his statements are correct, 'except on the one point--one of *form* not of *substance*--that of the address of the letter in which Mr. Crookes attested the genuineness of the mediumship of Eva Fay!'

It thus appears that, when he wrote the article in last month's *Fraser*, and the letter in *Nature* of October 25, Dr. Carpenter had not seen either the *fac-simile* letter or the account in the *Spiritualist*, and there is nothing to show that he even knew of the existence of the latter article; yet on the strength of mere rumour, newspaper cuttings, or imagination, he gives the supposed contents of a letter from Mr. Crookes, emphasising such obnoxious words as 'Spiritualistic' and 'manifestations,' which Mr. Crookes never once employed, and giving a totally false impression of what Mr. Crookes had really done. So enamoured is he of this accusation, that he drags it into a purely scientific discussion on the Radiometer, and now, in his very latest communication, makes no apology or retractation, but maintains all his statements as correct '*in substance*,' and declares that he 'cannot see that he has anywhere passed beyond the tone of gentlemanly discussion.'

Notes Appearing in the Original Work:

[1]Mr. Home has always been treated by Dr. Carpenter as an impostor: yet now he quotes him as an authority, although Mr. Home's accusations against other mediums are never authenticated in any way, and appear to be in many

cases pure imagination. Dr. Carpenter will no doubt now disclaim any imputation against Mr. Home, and pretend to consider him only as the victim of delusion. But this is absurd. For does he not maintain that Mr. Home was never 'levitated,' although in several cases the fact was proved by his name being found written in pencil on the ceiling where it remained? This must have been imposture if the levitation were not, as claimed, a reality. Do not the hands, other than those of any persons present, which have often appeared at Mr. Home's *séances* and have been visible and even tangible to all present, prove (in Dr. Carpenter's opinion) imposture? Do not the red-hot coals carried about the room in his hands prove chemical preparation, and therefore imposture? Is not the increase or decrease of the weight of a table, as ascertained by a spring-balance, which I have myself witnessed in Mr. Home's presence, a trick, according to Dr. Carpenter? Is not the playing of the accordion in one hand, or when both Mr. Home's hands are on the table, a clever imposture in Dr. Carpenter's opinion? But if any one of these things is admitted to be, not an imposture, but a reality, then the whole foundation of the learned but most illogical Doctor's scepticism is undermined, and he practically admits himself a convert to the *facts* of modern spiritualism. But he does *not* admit this; and as Mr. Home has carried on these alleged impostures during his whole life, and has imbued thousands of persons with a belief in their genuineness, Dr.

Carpenter must inevitably believe Mr. Home to be the vilest of impostors and utterly untrustworthy. Yet he quotes him as an authority, accepts as true all the malicious stories retailed by this alleged impostor against rival impostors, and believes every vague and entirely unsupported statement to a like effect in Mr. Home's last book! This from an ex-Professor of Medical Jurisprudence, who ought to have some rudimentary notions of the value of evidence, is truly surprising. It may be said that, although Dr. Carpenter thinks Home an impostor, *we* believe in him, and therefore ought to accept his evidence against other mediums. But this is a fallacy. We believe that he is a *medium*, that is, a machine or organisation *through* whom certain abnormal and marvellous phenomena occur; but this implies no belief in his integrity or in his judgment, any more than the extraordinary phenomenon of double individuality exhibited in the case of the French sergeant (which formed the subject of such an interesting article by Professor Huxley some time ago) implies that the sergeant was a man of high moral character and superior judgment. at the bottom of p and 696

[2] See *Nature*, Nov. 1, 1877, . on
[3] *Quarterly Journal of Science*, January 1872: 'A Reply to the Quarterly Review.' on
[4] See *Quarterly Journal of Science*, July 1877, p -412. on
[5] *Miracles and Modern Spiritualism*, . on

[6]Dr. Carpenter's *Mental Physiology*, 2nd edit. . on

[7]'In the United States more especially . . . the names of the "eminent British scientists," Messrs. Crookes and Wallace, are a "tower of strength." And it consequently becomes necessary for me to undermine that tower by showing that in their investigation of this subject they have followed methods that are thoroughly unscientific, and have been led, by their "prepossession," to accept with implicit faith a number of statements which ought to be rejected as completely untrustworthy.' --*Fraser's Magazine*, November 1877, . on

[8]The account in the *New York Daily Graphic* almost proves that they were not. For the clever woodcuts showing Mr. Bishop during his performances indicate an amount of stretching of the cord which certainly could be at once detected on after examination, especially if the knots had been sealed or bound with court-plaster. Yet more; according to these illustrations, it would be *impossible* for Mr. Bishop to imitate Eva Fay in 'tying a strip of cloth round her neck' and 'putting a ring into her ear,' both of which are specially mentioned as having been done by her. It may well be supposed that the audience, delighted at an 'exposure,' would not be quite so severely critical as they are to those who claim to possess abnormal powers.   on

[9]As hardly any of my readers will have seen the full account of these tests, and as the whole is too long for

insertion here, I give a pretty full abstract of all the essential portions of it in an Appendix to this paper. This is rendered necessary because Dr. Carpenter declares that he is going to give, in the new edition of his Lectures, 'the whole explanation' of the 'dodge' by which these 'scientific tests' could be evaded--'a dodge *so simple* that Mr. Crookes' highly-trained scientific acumen could not detect it.' These are Dr. Carpenter's own words in his article last month ( ), and it is necessary that he should be called on to make them good by really explaining Mr. Crookes' actual experiments, and not some other experiments which 'American newspapers' may substitute for them.   on
[10]*Quarterly Journal of Science*, Oct. 1871 and Jan. 1874. on

THE CURIOSITIES OF CREDULITY

(S285: 1878)

Owing to absence from home I have only just seen Dr. Carpenter's letter in the *Athenæum* of December 22nd, to which I now beg leave very briefly to reply.

I must first remark on the extreme inconvenience of Dr. Carpenter's erratic mode of carrying on a discussion. As soon as his lectures on 'Mesmerism, Spiritualism, &c.,' were published, I wrote a review of them in the *Quarterly Journal of Science* of July last. To this Dr. Carpenter replied in *Fraser's Magazine* of November, promising a fuller reply to certain points in the new edition of his 'Lectures,' then in the press. As the article in *Fraser* was of a very personal character, I issued a rejoinder in the same periodical the following month. A discussion has also been carried on in *Nature*, and the scene of the contest is now removed to the *Athenæum*, many of whose readers are probably ignorant of its previous phases.

Dr. Carpenter comes before a fresh audience in order

to reply to a specific charge of mis-statement which I made against him in the *Quarterly Journal of Science* (July, 1877,), which charge, as I will proceed to show, he endeavours to evade by a wordy defence, which really amounts to an admission of it. In his 'Lectures' ( ) is the following passage:--

"It was in France that the pretensions of mesmeric clairvoyance were first advanced; and it was by the French Academy of Medicine, in which the mesmeric state had been previously discussed with reference to the performance of surgical operations, that this new and more extraordinary claim was first carefully sifted, in consequence of an offer made in 1837 by M. Burdin (himself a member of that Academy) of a prize of 3,000 francs to any one who should be found capable of reading through opaque substances. The money was deposited in the hands of a notary for a period of two years, afterwards extended to three; the announcement was extensively published; numerous cases were offered for examination; every imaginable concession was made to the competitors that was compatible with a thorough testing of the asserted power; and not one was found to stand the trial."

My readers will observe that this is deliberately stated to be the *first* time that clairvoyance was carefully sifted in France; yet it now appears that Dr. Carpenter perfectly well knew of the Commission of the same Academy about ten years earlier, which, after five years of most careful and elaborate experiments, gave a unanimous Report positively in favour of the reality of clairvoyance.

But Dr. Carpenter would have us believe that he studiously avoided all mention of this Report because it had been proved to be wholly founded on imposture or error; and he endeavours to establish this by giving a single hearsay case of a confession of imposture *on another person not even a member of the Commission!* I feel sure that the impression conveyed to the readers of Dr. Carpenter's letters would be that the case of alleged imposture by one of the mesmeric patients of MM. Georget and Rostan occurred to members of the Commission, and that the case had been examined by them and reported on as genuine. But this impression would be entirely erroneous. The members of the Commission, whose names are appended to the Report, are as follows: 1, Bourdois de la Motte (President); 2, Fouquier; 3, Gueneau de Mussy; 4, Guersent; 5, Itard; 6, Leroux; 7, Marc; 8, Thillaye; 9, Husson (Reporter). Against the voluminous and interesting details of this Report, its carefully repeated experiments, its cautious deductions, its amazing facts, not one particle of rebutting evidence is adduced. Yet Dr. Carpenter thought himself justified not only in ignoring its existence, but in giving his readers to understand, by an express form of words, that no such inquiry was ever made! This was the accusation I made against him, and the readers of the *Athenæum* can now judge as to the candour and sufficiency of the reply.

I must add a few words on the way in which Dr. Carpenter treats M. Rostan, "one of the ablest medical psychologists of his day." Dr. Carpenter states, as a fact, that, "when a second edition of the 'Dictionnaire de Médecine' came out in 1838, he (M. Rostan) withdrew the article he had contributed to the first"; and then, further on, it is stated that "M. Rostan, by his own confession," had been led away by cunning cheats in the matter of clairvoyance. Now I have always understood that M. Rostan was much annoyed at his article being superseded in the second edition of the Dictionnaire; and, as this is *à priori* probable, I require some direct evidence of Dr. Carpenter's assertion that he voluntarily withdrew it. This is the more necessary because the still more important and damaging statement--that M. Rostan made a "confession" that he had been led away by cunning cheats--is also given as a hearsay report without any reference or authority; and it looks very much as if Dr. Carpenter's logic had deduced the "confession" as an inference from the "withdrawal," no evidence whatever being offered for either of them. If this should really be the case, then the severest things I have said as to Dr. Carpenter's mode of carrying on this discussion will be more than justified.

Throughout my discussion of this subject with Dr. Carpenter I have strictly confined myself to questions of *fact* and of *evidence*, and have maintained that these are of more value than *opinions*, however numerous or weighty. My criticisms have, for the most part, been directed to misrepresentations of facts and suppressions of evidence on the part of my opponent. The readers of the *Athenæum* will now be able to judge, as regards one case, whether that criticism is sound; and for numerous other cases I refer them to my articles in the *Quarterly Journal of Science* and in *Fraser's Magazine*. If they read these, they will, I think, agree with me that the cause of truth will not be advanced by the further continuance of a discussion in which one of the parties perpetually evades or obscures the most important points at issue, and at every step introduces fresh mis-statements to be corrected and fresh insinuations to be rebutted, as I have shown that Dr. Carpenter has done in his numerous writings on this subject.

PSYCHOLOGICAL CURIOSITIES OF CREDULITY

Dr. Carpenter's letter in your last issue so entirely fails to meet the allegations in my communication to the *Athenæum* of January the 12th, that I should be content to let the matter rest. But Dr. Carpenter now makes fresh statements, which I maintain to be both inaccurate and misleading, and I therefore ask permission to point them out.

In the first place, it is untrue that I have ever "required" Dr. Carpenter "and every one else" to have "full faith" in the Academic Report of 1830. My sole objection was to Dr. Carpenter's ignoring its very existence. It is also untrue that the French Academy of Medicine "deliberately reversed the judgment" of its first Commission, "as having been obtained by fraud and chicanery." The second and third Commissions were of more limited scope than the first; their conclusions were mostly negative; and neither they nor the Academy itself in any way pronounced judgment on the first Commission, as Dr. Carpenter's words imply that they did. The subject having thus been again brought to the notice of your readers, I beg leave to offer a few remarks on the nature of the investigation by the first Commission of the French

Academy of Medicine, and on the value of the evidence it affords.

We may certainly assume that the members of this Commission fairly represented the best medical talent of France at that time, for they were chosen by a representative society of doctors, who would carefully select men of exceptional acuteness, caution, and judgment, to investigate a subject about which there was so much dispute as mesmerism, or, as it was then termed, magnetism. That the members of the Commission were quite aware of the chief sources of error, and were not led away by any contagious enthusiasm, is evident from their Report itself. Thus, they declare that many of the effects ascribed to magnetism are produced by "expectation," "ennui," and by "the imagination"; that the effects are "very varied in different individuals"; and that some of the phenomena may be simulated and "furnish charlatanism with the means of deception." It is interesting to note that the patient first submitted to examination by M. Foissac (on whose proposition the Commission was appointed) turned out a complete failure; and had the Commission been hasty in arriving at conclusions, its report might have been as adverse to mesmerism as those which succeeded it. But the inquiry was continued, and other patients were found who submitted to every possible test. Finally, the members who attended the experiments, nine in number, *unanimously reported,* *after five years of inquiry,* "that magnetization without the knowledge of the patient; pre-vision of organic phenomena; knowledge of the internal condition of other persons; and true clairvoyance, had been demonstrated to them." One of the somnambulists determined correctly the symptoms of M. Marc, a Commissioner; and also the disease of another person, the accuracy of the diagnosis being confirmed by *post mortem* examination. Clairvoyance was proved by one of the patients repeatedly reading and naming cards, while four of the Commissioners successively held his eyes closed with their fingers,--a test, the absolute conclusiveness of which every one may satisfy himself of. These are mere illustrations from among dozens of similar cases.*

Now are we to believe that nine eminent medical men, investigating this subject at great length, and reporting on it with a full sense of responsibility, could possibly have been the victims of imposture and delusion throughout the whole inquiry, without any one of the nine so much as suspecting its possibility? That they had full confidence in their facts is shown by the following extract from the concluding portion of their Report:--

"Certainly we dare not flatter ourselves that we shall make you share entirely our conviction of the reality of the phenomena which we have observed, and which you have neither seen, nor followed, nor studied with or in opposition to us. We do not, therefore, exact from you a blind belief in all that we have reported. We conceive that a great part of the facts are so extraordinary that you cannot grant it to us; perhaps we ourselves should have refused you our belief, if, changing places, you had come to announce them before this tribunal to us, who, like you at present, had seen nothing, observed nothing, studied nothing, followed nothing of them."

Dr. Carpenter wholly disbelieves the facts and conclusions of the Commission, as well as the whole mass of subsequent confirmatory testimony. This he is quite free to do, without any objection on my part. I only object to his first denying (by implication) the very existence of the Report, and then giving illogical and inadequate reasons for so doing. These so-called reasons are, that the Academy did not formally adopt the Report; that two subsequent Commissions *failed* to obtain confirmatory evidence, and *did* detect some attempts at imposture; and that a woman made a death-bed confession that she had, in some unexplained way, tricked two doctors who were not members of either of the Commissions.

But the first Commission also had "failures"; it also recognized "imposture" or attempts at imposture; but besides these it obtained absolutely conclusive facts, which have subsequently been often confirmed, but have never been satisfactorily explained away. To take the ground that clairvoyance is altogether impossible, and therefore incredible on any evidence, would be an intelligible position; but to admit that it is a question of evidence, and then to reject such direct, positive, and weighty evidence as that of the Commission of 1825-31 on the mere negative grounds above referred to, is utterly unintelligible; for to do so is to place ignorance above knowledge, and to estimate negative as superior to positive results.

Note Appearing in the Original Work

*The Report is given at length in the 'Archives Générales de Médecine,' vol. XX., and is well worthy of careful perusal.

ARE THE PHENOMENA OF SPIRITUALISM IN HARMONY WITH SCIENCE?

(S379: 1885)

"Life is the elaboration of soul through the varied transformations of matter." --*Spiritual Evolution.*

It is a common, but I believe a mistaken, notion, that the conclusions of Science are antagonistic to the alleged phenomena of modern Spiritualism. The majority of our teachers and students of science are, no doubt, antagonistic, but their opinions and prejudices are not science. Every discoverer who has promulgated new and startling truths, even in the domain of physics, has been denounced or ignored by those who represented the science of the day, as witness the long line of great teachers from Galileo in the dark ages to Boucher de Perthes in our own times. But the opponents of Spiritualism have the additional advantage of being able to brand the new belief as a degrading superstition, and to accuse those who accept its facts and its teachings of being the victims of delusion or imposture--

of being, in fact, either half-insane enthusiasts or credulous fools. Such denunciations, however, affect us little. The fact that Spiritualism has firmly established itself in our sceptical and materialistic age, that it has continuously grown and developed for nearly forty years, that by mere weight of evidence, and in spite of the most powerful prepossessions, it has compelled recognition by an ever-increasing body of men in all classes of society, and has gained adherents in the highest ranks of science and philosophy, and, finally, that despite abuse and misrepresentation, the folly of enthusiasts and the knavery of impostors, it has rarely failed to convince those who have made a thorough and painstaking investigation, and has never lost a convert thus made--all this affords a conclusive answer to the objections so commonly urged against it. Let us, then, simply ignore the scorn and incredulity of those who really know nothing of the matter, and consider, briefly, what are the actual relations of Science and Spiritualism, and to what extent the latter supplements and illumines the former.

Science may be defined as knowledge of the universe in which we live--full and systematised knowledge leading to the discovery of laws and the comprehension of causes. The true student of science neglects nothing and despises nothing that may widen and deepen his knowledge of nature, and if he is wise as well as learned he will hesitate before he applies the term "impossible" to any facts which are widely believed and have been repeatedly observed by men as intelligent and honest as himself. Now, modern Spiritualism rests solely on the observation and comparison of facts in a domain of nature which has been hitherto little explored, and it is a contradiction in terms to say that such an investigation is opposed to science. Equally absurd is the allegation that some of the phenomena of Spiritualism "contradict the laws of nature," since there is no law of nature yet known to us but may be apparently contravened by the action of more recondite laws or forces. Spiritualists observe facts and record experiments, and then construct hypotheses which will best explain and co-ordinate the facts, and in so doing they are pursuing a truly scientific course. They have now collected an enormous body of observations tested and verified in every possible way, and they have determined many of the conditions necessary for the production of the phenomena. They have also arrived at certain general conclusions as to the causes of these phenomena, and they simply refuse to recognise the competence of those who have no acquaintance whatever with the facts, to determine the value or correctness of those conclusions.

We who have satisfied ourselves of the reality of the phenomena of modern Spiritualism in all their wide-reaching extent and endless variety, are enabled to look upon the records of the past with new interest and fuller appreciation. It is surely something to be relieved from the necessity of classing Socrates and St. Augustine, Luther and Swedenborg, as the credulous victims of delusion or imposture. The so-called miracles and supernatural events which pervade the sacred books and historical records of all nations find their place among natural phenomena, and need no longer be laboriously explained away. The witchcraft mania of Europe and America affords the materials for an important study, since we are now able to detect the basis of fact on which it rested, and to separate from it the Satanic interpretation which invested it with horror, and appeared to justify the cruel punishments by which it was attempted to be suppressed. Local folk-lore and superstitions acquire a living interest, since they are often based on phenomena which we can reproduce under proper conditions, and the same may be said of much of the sorcery and magic of the Middle Ages. In these and many other ways history and anthropology are illuminated by Spiritualism.

To the teacher of religion it is of vital importance, since it enables him to meet the sceptic on his own ground, to adduce facts and evidence for the faith that he professes, and to avoid that attitude of apology and doubt which renders him altogether helpless against the vigorous assaults of Agnosticism and materialistic science. Theology, when vivified and strengthened by Spiritualism, may regain some of the influence and power of its earlier years.

Science will equally benefit, since it will have opened

to it a new domain of surpassing interest. Just as there is behind the visible world of nature an "unseen universe" of forces, the study of which continually opens up fresh worlds of knowledge often intimately connected with the true comprehension of the most familiar phenomena of nature, so the world of mind will be illuminated by the new facts and principles which the study of Spiritualism makes known to us. Modern science utterly fails to realize the nature of mind or to account for its presence in the universe, except by the mere verbal and unthinkable dogma that it is "the product of organization." Spiritualism, on the other hand, recognises in Mind the cause of organization, and, perhaps, even of matter itself; and it has added greatly to our knowledge of man's nature, by demonstrating the existence of individual minds indistinguishable from those of human beings, yet separate from any human body. It has made us acquainted with forms of matter of which materialistic science has no cognizance, and with an ethereal chemistry whose transformations are far more marvellous than any of those with which science deals. It thus gives us proof that there are possibilities of organized existence beyond those of our material world, and in doing so removes the greatest stumbling-block in the way of belief in a future state of existence--the impossibility so often felt by the student of material science of separating the conscious mind from its partnership with the brain and nervous system.

On the spiritual theory man consists essentially of a spiritual nature or mind intimately associated with a spiritual body or soul, both of which are developed in and by means of a material organism. Thus the whole *raison d'être* of the material universe--with all its marvellous changes and adaptations, the infinite complexity of matter and of the ethereal forces which pervade and vivify it, the vast wealth of nature in the vegetable and animal kingdoms--is to serve the grand purpose of developing human spirits in human bodies.

This world-life not only lends itself to the production, by gradual evolution, of the physical body needed for the growth and nourishment of the human soul, but by its very imperfections tends to the continuous development of the higher spiritual nature of man. In a perfect and harmonious world perfect beings might possibly have been created but could hardly have been evolved, and it may well be that evolution is the great fundamental law of the universe of mind as well as of that of matter. The need for labour in order to live, the constant struggle against the forces of nature, the antagonism of the good and the bad, the oppression of the weak by the strong, the painstaking and devoted search required to wrest from nature her secret powers and hidden treasures--all directly assist in developing the varied powers of mind and body and the nobler impulses of our nature. Thus, all the material imperfections of our globe, the wintry blasts and summer heats, the volcano, the whirlwind and the flood, the barren desert and the gloomy forest, have each served as *stimuli* to develop and strengthen man's intellectual nature; while the oppression and wrong, the ignorance and crime, the misery and pain, that always and everywhere pervade the world, have been the means of exercising and strengthening the higher sentiments of justice, mercy, charity, and love, which we all feel to be our best and noblest characteristics, and which it is hardly possible to conceive could have been developed by any other means.*

Such a view as this affords us the best attainable solution of the great world-old problem of the origin of evil; for it is the very means of creating and developing the higher moral attributes of man, those attributes which alone render him fit for a permanent spiritual existence and for continuous progression, then the mere temporary sin and misery of the world must be held to be fully justified by the supreme nature and permanent character of what they lead to. From this point of view the vision of the poet becomes to us the best expression of the truth. We, too, believe that

"All Nature is but Art, unknown to thee;
All Chance, Direction which thus canst not see;
All Discord, Harmony not understood;
All partial Evil, universal Good."

Finally, these teachings of modern Spiritualism furnish us with the much-needed basis of a true ethical system. We learn by them that our earth-life is not only a preparation for a higher state of progressive spiritual existence, but that what we have usually considered as its very worst features, its all-pervading sin and suffering, are in all probability the only means of developing in us those highest moral qualities summarized as "love" by St. Paul and "altruism" by our modern teachers, which all admit must be cultivated and extended to the utmost if we are really to make progress toward a higher social state. Modern philosophers can, however, give no sufficient reason why we should practise these virtues. If, as they teach us, not only our own lives end here, but the life of the whole human race is sure to end some day, it is difficult to see any adequate outcome of the painful self-sacrifice they inculcate; while there is certainly no motive adduced which will be sufficiently powerful to withdraw from selfish pleasures that numerous class which derives from them its chief enjoyment. But when men are taught from childhood that the whole material universe exists for the very purpose of developing beings possessing these attributes, that evil and pain, sin and suffering, all tend to the same end, and that the characters developed in this world will make further progress towards a nobler and happier existence in the spiritual world, just in proportion as their higher moral feelings are cultivated here--and when all this can be taught, not as a set of dogmas to be blindly accepted on the authority of unknown ancient writers, but as being founded on direct knowledge of the spirit-world, and the continued actual reception of teachings from it, then indeed we shall have in our midst "a power that makes for righteousness."

Thus, modern Spiritualism, though usually despised and rejected by the learned, is yet able to give valuable aid to science and to religion, to philosophy and to morals. Not only does it offer us a solid basis for a solution of some of the profoundest mysteries of our being, but it affords us a secure hope, founded not on reason and faith only, but on actual knowledge, that our conscious life does not perish with our physical body. To all who will earnestly inquire it gives:--

"The deep assurance that the wrongs of life
Will find their perfect guerdon! That the scheme
So broken here will elsewhere be fulfilled!
Hope not a dreamer's dream!
Love's long last yearnings satisfied, not stilled!"

Note Appearing in the Original Work
*This argument applies of course to other worlds and systems, all of which, on the spiritual hypothesis, either have been or will be the scenes of the development of human souls. on

THE "JOURNAL OF SCIENCE" ON SPIRITUALISM

(S382: 1885)

My article on the "Harmony of Spiritualism and Science," written for an American newspaper, and republished in "Light" of May 30th, has been honoured by a notice in the *Journal of Science,* and I have been requested to make a few remarks in reply to the same. I cannot say that I myself think the criticism worth answering, because it is founded on assumptions which will, I am sure, not be granted by men of science in general; still, as they may present difficulties to some readers, it is perhaps as well to show their weakness.

The writer's main and fundamental objection is stated as follows:--

"Science is based upon what we, for want of a better name, term *law.* Spiritualism rests upon *will.* Science, and not merely our present science, but any possible science, so far as I can conceive it--takes its stand upon the causal nexus, upon the regular sequence of cause and effect. Iron always sinks in mercury, and always dissolves in hydrochloric acid, &c., &c." . . .

In this passage and in what follows, the term "science" is completely misused. It is taken as synonymous with a limited branch of science, namely--physics. There are, however, whole regions of science in which there is no such regular sequence of cause and effect and no power of prediction. Even within the domain of physics we have the science of meteorology in which there is no precise sequence of effects; and when we came to the more complex phenomena of life we can rarely predict results and are continually face to face with insoluble problems; yet no one maintains that meteorology and biology are not sciences--still less that they are out of harmony with or opposed to science. The absence of uniformity, and the impossibility of predicting what will happen under all circumstances are not, therefore, confined to Spiritualistic phenomena alone. Assuming that they are so, however, the writer thus continues:--

"With the advent of Spiritualism all this beautiful simplicity has been swept away. If Spiritualists are not mistaken there are around us numbers of finite invisible beings, of unknown powers, and of unknown intentions capable of interfering with the order of nature. They can raise bodies in the air against the force of gravitation. They can kindle fires at pleasure, or deprive fire of the power of destroying organised beings or of occasioning pain. . . . To me it seems that, if these contentions are true, if there exist beings around us capable of exerting such powers, there are introduced, so to speak, into every equation a number of unknown quantities, rendering it for ever insoluble. We can only say 'such results will follow under such conditions, if no spirits think proper to interfere.' It seems to me that before any harmony can be shown between Spiritualism and science it must be ascertained what are the limits of the powers of these 'spirits' and under what conditions can they be exerted. In that manner only can a basis for science be saved."

In this passage there are both misstatements of fact and illogical conclusions. There is little or no proof that the "spirits" around us can of *themselves* do any of the things alleged. They require in almost every case, perhaps in every case, the assistance of human beings, and not only so, but of particular human beings with special organisations--those we term mediums. Here at once is a limitation to their power, and so great a limitation that the cases in which they can interfere with the ordinary effects of natural law are but very rare exceptions. Unless specially sought after, not one person in a thousand ever comes in contact with these phenomena, and even when sought for the general complaint is that they are exceedingly hard to find. To maintain that all science is impossible because once or twice in the lives of one person in a thousand some interference with the ordinary course of nature may occur, is about as sensible as to maintain that agriculture is impossible because phenomenal hailstorms may destroy, or exceptional whirlwinds may carry away, crops, or to give up all quantitative astronomical observation because earthquakes or terrestrial tremors, which cannot be predicted, may alter the level or the orientation of the instruments. And when we come to vital, and mental, and moral phenomena, we are still more subject to "unknown quantities in our equations." The apparently healthy man dies suddenly, while one who has always been weak and ailing lives to a good old age. The sober, moral, and religious citizen suddenly commits a horrible crime. The man of commanding genius becomes hopelessly insane. Yet these terribly real "unknown quantities" do not render either vital, or mental, or moral science impossible, still less do they place these studies altogether outside of science and in antagonism to it.

Again, as regards the impossibility of any science, as the critic alleges, where *will* intervenes, we have the human will as a constant factor in sociology, in anthropology, in ethical science, in history, in psychology, yet no one maintains that all these studies are opposed to science even if they have, as yet, no claim to rank among established or exact sciences.

Now, so far as we know, the *will* of spirits is no more erratic in its manifestations than the will of living men. It appears to be equally subject to general laws and influences, and, on the average, no more affects the orderly sequence of Spiritualistic phenomena than do the individual wills of human beings affect the orderly sequence of mental, social, or moral phenomena. It is a great mistake to impute all the uncertainty of phenomena with mediums to the erratic *will* of the spirits concerned. Very little is probably due to this cause, while the greater part is certainly owing to what may strictly be termed terrestrial conditions. We know something of these conditions already, and when we know more we have every reason to believe that much of the uncertainty will cease. Not less unsatisfactory is the remark with which our critic concludes this part of the subject:--

"To harmonise science with Spiritualism it will then be, in the first place, necessary to discover the limits of the power of spirits, under what conditions it is exerted, and how it may be combated when and where it is desirable."

But in all these respects Spiritualism is fully as advanced as is science itself. We know, practically, the limits of the power of spirits on this earth at the present day, and under ordinary conditions, quite as well as we know the limits of the power of earthquakes and volcanoes, of disease, of insanity, and of human intellect, and we know how to combat their evil effects quite as well in our domain of observation as do men of science in theirs.

Then we have the bugbear of the "creation or destruction of energy" in Spiritualistic phenomena brought forward, and we are told that scientific men will seek for "precise answers" to the question where the power comes from "before they can accept the Spiritualistic theories." But nobody asks them to accept the Spiritualist theories before they have investigated the Spiritualist facts.

It has usually been the boast of science that it accepts, and co-ordinates, and studies *all* the facts of nature in order to explain them; but with respect to our facts it applies a different rule and asks for a complete theory--a "precise explanation," before it will even begin to study them. We are informed that, in order--"To establish a harmony between Spiritualism and science it will be necessary, I submit, to show the origin of the energy which is at the disposal of spirits." But science itself does not yet know the "origin of the energy" of gravitation, yet the theory of gravitation is its proudest boast. Science only guesses at the "origin of the energy" of the magnet; and in tracing all terrestrial energy to the sun it only removes the difficulty one step, and cannot do more than make more or less probable guesses as to where the energy of the sun comes form. It is surely not scientific to demand of a new and very difficult science the complete solution of its most fundamental problems as a preliminary to recognising its existence, yet this is how the writer in the *Journal of Science* proposes to treat the students of Spiritualism.

The last passage I shall refer to is that in which the critic considers that Swedenborg was the victim "of delusion or imposture," because, while describing Jupiter and Saturn he said nothing about Uranus or Neptune. The assumption underlying this argument is, that if spirits exist and communicate with men they *must necessarily* know more of the material universe than men do, and *must* communicate their superior knowledge to us. This extraordinary misconception well illustrates the tone of mind of the writer, who has evidently given very little attention to the theories and conclusions of the more advanced of modern Spiritualists. He has yet to learn that the facts of Spiritualism are one thing, the value of the information obtained from Spiritualistic sources quite another thing. It is marvellous that so many people who deny that we have any evidence whatever of the existence of spirits, yet claim to know *à priori* exactly what spirits ought to know and ought to tell us, if they do exist!

THE HARMONY OF SPIRITUALISM AND SCIENCE

(S383: 1885)

I find some difficulty in comprehending the exact position of Mr. Frederick F. Cook in his elaborate "Rejoinder" to my article, but with your permission I will briefly notice his direct criticisms of my views, because they have a certain amount of plausibility owing to the extremely condensed form in which I was compelled to express myself in the space that was allowed me.

Mr. Cook first objects to my proposition that--"man consists essentially of a spiritual nature or mind intimately associated with a spiritual body or soul, both of which are developed in, and by means of, a material organism." This, he says, is a case of spiritual suicide, and is directly opposed to my previous statement that--"mind is the cause of organism and perhaps even of matter itself." But surely, it is clear that in the last quoted passage I am speaking of mind in the

214

abstract or as a fundamental principle, while in the former I am dealing with mind as individualised in the human form. There is, I conceive, no contradiction in believing that mind is at once the cause of matter and of the development of individualised human minds through the agency of matter. And when, further on, he asks, "Does mortality give consciousness to spirit, or does spirit give consciousness for a limited period to mortality?" I would reply, "Neither the one nor the other; but, mortality is the means by which a permanent individuality is given to spirit."

His next serious objection is to my supposition that, "it may well be that evolution is a fundamental law of the universe of mind as well as that of matter." This, he says, is a purely materialistic thought. But here again it is clear by the context that I am referring solely to the development of individualised human minds, of which alone we know, or can know, anything, not to mind in the abstract, of which we know absolutely nothing; and I see no materialism in the supposition that such finite individualised minds can only be produced under some law of evolution.

The last special criticism refers to my belief that "progress towards a nobler and happier existence in the spiritual world" is dependent on the cultivation of our higher moral feelings here. My critic says that this is an utter denial of justice or equality, because our moral nature, as well as our environment, is imposed upon us; but he does not say whether he accepts the alternative position, that all are to be at once good and happy in the future state, and that the most selfish, vicious, and sensual are to make equal progress with the benevolent, self-sacrificing, and virtuous. It seems to me that this latter condition of things would be the most opposed to justice, and even to possibility, and would render the present world, with all its trials, a hopeless and insoluble mystery, while it is certainly opposed to the whole body of information and teaching which we receive from spiritual sources.

It seems to me that my critic, throughout, confuses together the general with the special, the universal with the individual, in discussing the relations of spirit and matter, while he equally confounds proximate with ultimate results in his remarks on the spiritual world. My observations and reasonings have been confined throughout to the nature and relations of individualised human minds and their proximate condition in the spirit world. Speculations on the nature or origin of mind in general as well as those on the ultimate states to which human minds may attain in the infinite future, I look upon as altogether beyond the range of our faculties, and to be, therefore, utterly untrustworthy and profitless.

WHAT ARE PHANTASMS, AND WHY DO THEY APPEAR?

(S434: 1891)

The theories which have been suggested by the more prominent members of the Society for Psychical Research in order to explain the phenomena of phantasms or apparitions of various kinds, are all founded on telepathy, or thought-transference, the facts of which have been demonstrated by a long series of experiments. It is found that many persons are more or less sensitive to the thoughts or will-powers of others, and are able to reproduce, more or less closely, any definite mental images sought to be conveyed to them. It is urged that those who experience phantasmal sights or sounds are a kind of thought-readers, and are so powerfully affected by the thoughts of friends who are in certain excitable mental states or physical crises, especially at periods of imminent danger or when at the point of death, as to externalize those thoughts in visual or auditory hallucinations either in the waking state or as unusually vivid dreams.

This telepathic theory is held to receive strong support, and in fact to be almost proved, by the curious phenomena of the doubles, or phantasms, of living persons being seen by certain sensitive friends, when those persons strongly *will* that they shall be so seen. Such are the cases of a friend appearing to Mr. Stainton Moses at a time when this friend had fixed his thoughts upon him before going to bed; and those of Mr. B__ who several times appeared in the night to two ladies, on occasions when he went to sleep with the express wish and intention of appearing to them.[1] There are, however, difficulties in these cases. The supposed agent does not usually decide exactly how he will appear or what he will do. In one case Mr. B__ appeared, not to the ladies he was thinking of, but a married sister, hardly known to him, who happened to be occupying their room. This lady saw the phantasm in the passage, going from one room to the other, at a time when the agent wished to be in the house; and again, the same night, at a time when he wished to be in the front bedroom, and on this occasion the phantasm came to her bedside and took hold of her hair, and then of her hand, gazing intently into it. Now it is an assumption hardly warranted by the facts, that the mere wish or determination to be in a certain part of a house at a certain time could cause a phantasm to appear to a person who happened unexpectedly to be there, and cause that phantasm to perform, or appear to perform, certain acts which do not appear to have been *willed* by the supposed agent. This is certainly not telepathy in the usually accepted sense; it is not the transference of a thought to an individual, but the production of what seems to be an objective phantasm in a definite locality. It is altogether inconceivable, that a mere wish could produce such a phantasm, unless, indeed, we suppose the spirit of the sleeper to leave the body in order to go to the desired place, and that it possesses the power to render itself visible to anyone who happens to be there. Let us then see whether there are any other facts concerning doubles which may throw some light on this question.

Mr. Fryer, of Bath, England, heard his name distinctly called in the voice of a brother who had been some days absent from home. At the same moment, as near as could be ascertained, the brother missed his footing and fell on a railway platform, calling out his brother's name as he fell.[2] Similar in character is the case of Mrs. Severn, who, while in bed one morning, felt a violent blow on her lip so real that she put her handkerchief to it, expecting to find it bleeding. At the same time Mr. Severn, caught by a squall in a boat, received a violent blow on the same part of his mouth from the tiller. In the first case, Mr. Fryer's brother had no conscious wish to be heard by him; and in the other case, Mr. Severn certainly did not wish his wife to feel the blow, but, on the contrary, was extremely anxious to conceal from her that he had had a blow at all.[3] In both these cases, if the supposed agents had anything to do with the actual production of the phantasmal voice and sensation, it was by some unconscious or automatic process. But the experimental evidence for telepathy shows it to be produced by the conscious and active will-power of the agent or agents, and would therefore prove, if anything, that in both these cases there was some third party who was really the agent in willing and producing the telepathic effect. This is rendered still more probable by other cases of "doubles" and of warnings, of which the following is one of the most remarkable.

Mr. Algernon Joy, an engineer employed on the Penarth Docks, at Cardiff, South Wales, was walking in a country lane near the town, absorbed in a calculation connected with the Docks, when he was attacked and knocked down by two young colliers. His thoughts were then immediately directed to the possible cause of the attack, to the possibility of identifying the men, and to informing the police. He is positive that for about half an hour previous to the attack and for an hour or two after it, there was no connection whatever, direct or indirect, between his thoughts and a friend in London. Yet at almost the precise moment of the assault, this friend recognized Mr. Joy's footstep in the street, behind him, then turned and saw Mr. Joy "as distinctly as ever he saw him in his life," saw he looked distressed, asked what was the matter, and received the answer, "Go home, old fellow, I've been hurt." All this was communicated in a letter from the friend which crossed one from Mr. Joy, giving an account of the accident.[4] In this case, whether the "double" was an audible and visual veridical hallucination, or an objective phantasm, it could not have been produced without some adequate cause. To assert that Mr. Joy was himself the unconscious cause cannot be looked upon as an explanation, or as in any way helping us to a comprehension of how such things can happen. We imperatively need a producing agent, some intellectual being having both the will and the power to produce such a veridical phantasm.

The next case still more clearly demands an agent other than that of any of the parties immediately concerned. Mr. F. Morgan, of Bristol, a young man who lived with his mother, was attending a lecture in which he was much interested. On entering the lecture room he saw a friend, with whom he determined to walk home after the lecture. About the middle of the lecture he noticed a door at the side of the platform farthest from the entrance to the hall, and he suddenly, without knowing why, got up and walked half the length of the hall to see if the door would open. He turned the handle, entered, and closed the door behind him, finding himself in the dark under the platform. Noticing a glimmer of light he went towards it, got into a passage which led again into the hall, the end of which he crossed to the entrance door, without any thought of the lecture which was still going on, or of the friend with whom he had meant to return, and then walked home quietly, without any excitement or impression of any kind, and quite unconscious till long after that he had done anything unusual. When he got home, however, he found that the house next to his was on fire and his mother in great alarm. He instantly removed his mother to a place of safety, and then had two or three hours' struggle with the flames. The adjoining house was burnt down, and his own was in great danger, and was slightly damaged.

Mr. Morgan states that his character is such that had he felt any impression that there was a fire, or that his mother was in danger, he should probably have shaken it off as mere fancy and refused to obey it. His mother simply wished for his presence, but exerted no will-power towards him. What agency, then, was it that acted upon his mental organization, at first apparently through simple curiosity, in such a strange yet effectual way, bringing him home so promptly, and yet without his feeling that he was in any way being influenced or guided in his actions, which seemed to himself to be perfectly voluntary and normal? We cannot avoid seeing in this case the continuous exercise of some mental influence, guided by accurate knowledge of the character of the individual and of his special surroundings at the moment, and directed with such care and judgment as to avoid exciting in him that antagonism which would have been fatal to the object aimed at. We see then that, even confining ourselves to undoubted phantasms of the living, or to impressions not connected with death, the facts are totally inexplicable on any theory of telepathy between living persons, but clearly point to the agency of preter-human intelligences--in other words, of spirits. The prejudice against such a conception is enormous, but the work of the Psychical Research Society has, it is to be hoped, somewhat undermined it. They have established, beyond further dispute for all who study the evidence, that veridical phantasms of the dead do exist; and the evidence itself--not ignorant or even scientific prejudice--must decide whether these phantasms which, as we have seen in my last article *i.e., S430* , are often objective, are the work of men or of spirits.

Before adducing further evidence on this point, it will be well to consider briefly, the extraordinary theory of the "second self" or "unconscious *ego,*" which is appealed to by many modern writers as a substitute for spirit agency when that of the normal human being is plainly inadequate. This theory is founded on the phenomena of dreams, of clairvoyance, and of duplex personality, and has been elaborately expounded by Du Prel in two volumes 8vo, translated by Mr. C. C. Massey. As an example of the kind of facts this theory is held to explain, we may refer to the experiments of the Rev. P. H. Newnham and Mrs. Newnham with planchette. The experiments were conducted by Mrs. N__ sitting at a low table with her hand on the planchette, while Mr. N__ sat with his back towards her at another table eight feet distant. Mr. N__ wrote questions on paper, and instantly, sometimes simultaneously, the planchette under Mrs. N__'s hand wrote the answers. Experiments were carried on for eight months, during which time three hundred and nine questions and answers were recorded. All kinds of questions were asked, and the answers were always pertinent to the questions though often evasions rather than direct answers. Great numbers of the answers did not correspond with the opinions or expectations of either Mr. or Mrs. N__, and were sometimes beyond their knowledge. To convince an incredulous visitor, Mr. N__ went with him into the hall, where he, the visitor, wrote down the question, "What is the Christian name of my eldest sister?" Mr. N__ saw the question but did not know the name, yet on returning to the study they found that planchette had already written "Mina," the family abbreviation of Wilhelmina, which was the correct name. Mr. N__ is a Free Mason, and asked many questions as to the Masonic ritual of which Mrs. N__ knew nothing. The answers were partly correct and partly incorrect, sometimes quite original, as when a prayer used at the advancement of a Mark Master Mason was asked for, and a very admirable prayer instantly written out, using Masonic terms, but, Mr. N__ says, quite unlike the actual prayer he was thinking of, and also unlike any prayer used by Masons or known to Mr. N__. It was in fact, as Mr. N__ says, "a formula composed by some intelligence totally distinct from the conscious intelligence of either of the persons engaged in the experiment."

Now all this, and a great deal more equally remarkable, is imputed to the agency of Mrs. Newnham's "unconscious self," a second independent, intelligent personality of which Mrs. Newnham herself knows nothing except when it "emerges" under special conditions, such as those here described. In the same way Du Prel explains all the phenomena of clairvoyance, of premonitions, of apparent possession, and of the innumerable cases in which sensitives exhibit knowledge of facts which in their normal state they do not possess, and have had no possible means of acquiring.

But is this so-called explanation any real explanation, or anything more than a juggle of words which creates more difficulties that it solves? The conception of such a double personality in each of us, a second self which in most cases remains unknown to us all our lives, which is said to live an independent mental life, to have means of acquiring knowledge our normal self does not possess, to exhibit all the characteristics of a distinct individuality with a different character from our own is surely a conception more ponderously difficult, more truly supernatural than that of a spirit-world, composed of beings who have lived, and learned, and suffered on earth, and whose mental nature still subsists after its separation from the earthly body. We shall find, too, that this latter theory explains *all* the facts simply and directly, that it is in accordance with *all* the evidence, and that in an overwhelming majority of cases, it is the explanation given by the communicating intelligences themselves. On the "second self" theory, we have to suppose that this recondite but worser half of ourselves, while possessing some knowledge we have not, does not know that it is part of us, or if it knows, is a persistent liar, for in most cases it adopts a distinct name, and persists in speaking of us, its better half, in the third person.

But there is yet another, and I think a more fundamental objection to this view, in the impossibility of conceiving how, or why, this second-self was developed in us under the law of survival of the fittest. The theory is upheld to avoid recourse to any "spiritual" explanation of phenomena, "spirit" being the last thing our modern men of science "will give in to."[5] But if so--if there is no spiritual nature in man that survives the earthly body, if man is but a highly intellectual animal developed from a lower animal form under the law of the survival of the fittest, how did this "second-self," this "unconscious *ego*," come into existence? Have the mollusk and the reptile, the dog and the ape, "unconscious *egos*"? And if so, why? And what use are they to these creatures, so that they might have been developed by means of the struggle for existence? Darwin detected no sign of such "second-selves" either in animals or men; and if they do not pertain to animals but do pertain to men, then we are involved in the same difficulty that is so often urged against spiritualists, that we require some break in the law of continuous development, and some exertion of a higher power to create and bring into the human organism this strange and useless "unconscious *ego*"--useless except to puzzle us with insoluble problems, and make our whole nature and existence seem more mysterious than ever. Of course this unconscious *ego* is supposed to die with the conscious man, for if not, we are introduced to a new and gratuitous difficulty, of the relation of these two intelligences and characters, distinct yet bound indissolubly together, in the after life.

Finding, therefore, that the theory of duplex personality creates more difficulties than it solves, while the facts it proposes to explain can be dealt with far more thoroughly on the spiritual hypothesis, let us pass on to consider the further evidence we possess for the agency of the spirits of the dead, or of some other preter-human intelligences.

We will first consider the case of Mrs. Menneer, who dreamed twice the same night, that she saw her headless brother standing at the foot of the bed with his head lying on a coffin by his side. She did not at the time know where her brother, Mr. Wellington, was, except that he was abroad. He was, however, at Sarawak, with Sir James Brooke, and was killed during the Chinese insurrection there, in a brave attempt to defend Mrs. Middleton and her children. Being taken for the Rajah's son, his head was cut off and carried away in triumph, his body being burned with the Rajah's house. The date of the dream coincided approximately with that of the death.[6] Now in this case it is almost certain that the head was cut off *after* death, since these Chinese were not trained soldiers, but gold miners, who would strike, and stab, and cut with any weapons they possessed, but could certainly not kill a European on his defence by cutting off his head at a blow. The impression on the sister's brain must, therefore, have been made either by the dead brother, or by some other intelligence, probably the latter, as it was clearly a symbolic picture, the head resting on the coffin showing that the head alone was recovered and buried. In a published letter of Sir James Brooke's he says--"Poor Wellington's remains were likewise consumed, his head borne off in triumph, *alone attesting* his previous murder."

Another case recorded in the same volume, is still more clear against the theory of telepathy between living persons. Mrs. Storie, of Edinburgh, living at the time in Hobart Town, Tasmania, one night dreamed a strange, confused dream, like a series of dissolving views. She saw her twin brother sitting in the open air, in the moonlight, sideways, on a raised place. Then he lifted his arm saying, "*The train, the train!*" Something struck him, he fell down fainting, a large dark object came by with a *swish*. Then she saw a railway compartment, in which sat a gentleman she knew, Rev. Mr. Johnstone. Then she saw her brother again. He put his right hand over his face as if in grief. Then a voice, not his voice, telling her he was going away. The same night her brother was killed by a train, having sat down to rest on the side of the track and fallen asleep. The details in the dream, of which the above is a bare abstract, were almost exactly as in the event, and the Mr. Johnstone of the dream was in the train that killed her brother. Now this last mentioned fact could not have been known to the dead man during life, and the dream-picture of the event must, therefore, have been due to the telepathic power of the dead man, or of some spirit-friend acquainted with the facts, and wishing to give a proof of spirit-life.

Take next the case of the Glasgow manufacturer settled in London, who dreams that one of his workmen in Glasgow, whom he had befriended as a lad, but with whom he had not had any direct relations for many years, comes to speak to him, begging him not to believe what he is accused of doing. On being asked what it is, he repeats three times, emphatically, "Ye'll sune ken." The dreamer also notices that the man has a remarkable appearance, bluish pale with great drops of sweat on his face. On awaking, his wife brings him a letter from his manager in Glasgow, telling him that this man, Robert Mackenzie, has committed suicide by drinking *aqua fortis*. The symptoms of poisoning by *aqua fortis* are those observed in the dream figure.[7] Here the man had died two days before the dream, which was just in time to correct the false impression of suicide that would have been produced by the letter. The whole of the features and details of the dream are such as could hardly have been due to any other agent than the dead workman himself, who was anxious that a master who had been kind to him when a lad, should not be led to credit the false accusation against him.

Dreams giving the details of funerals at a distance are not uncommon. As an example we have one in which Mr. Stainton Moses was invited to the funeral of a friend in Lincolnshire, but could not go. About the time of the funeral, however, he fell into a trance, and appeared to be at the ceremony, and on again becoming conscious, wrote down all the details, describing the clergyman, who was not the one who had been expected to officiate, the churchyard, which was at a distance in Northamptonshire, with a particular tree near the grave. He then sent this description to a friend who had been present, and who wrote back in astonishment as to how he could have obtained the details.[8] This may be said to be mere clairvoyance; but clairvoyance is a term that explains nothing, and is quite as mysterious and unintelligible if supposed to occur without the intervention of disembodied intelligences as if with their help. These cases also merge into others which are of a symbolical nature, and which clairvoyance of actual scenes at a distance cannot explain. A well-attested case of this kind is the following:

Philip Weld, a student at a Catholic College, was drowned in the river at Ware, Hertfordshire, in the year 1846. About the same hour as the accident, the young man's father and sister, while walking on the turnpike road near Southampton, saw him standing on the causeway with another young man in a black robe. The sister said, "Look, papa, there is Philip." Mr. Weld replied, "It is Philip indeed, but he has the look of an angel." They went on to embrace him, but before reaching him a laboring man seemed to walk through the figures, and then with a smile both figures vanished. The President of the College, Dr. Cox, went immediately to Southampton, to break the sad news to the father, but before he could speak, Mr. Weld told him what he had seen, and said he knew his son was dead. A few weeks afterwards, Mr. Weld visited the Jesuit College of Stonyhurst in Lancashire, and in the guest-room saw a picture of the very same young man he had seen with his son, similarly dressed, and in the same attitude, and beneath the picture was inscribed "St. Stanislaus Kotska," a saint of the Jesuit order who had been chosen by Philip for his patron saint at his confirmation.[2]

Now, here is a case in which phantasms of the son and of another person appear to two relatives, and the presence of the unknown person was eminently calculated, when his identity was discovered, to relieve the father's mind of all fear for his son's future happiness. It is hardly possible to have a clearer case of a true phantasm of the dead, not necessarily produced either *by* the dead son or the Jesuit saint, but most probably by them, or by some other spirit friend who had the power to produce such phantasms, and so relieve the anxiety of both father and sister. It is not conceivable that any living person's telepathic action could have produced such phantasms in two percipients, the only possible agent being the President of the College, who did not recognize by Mr. Weld's description, the dark-robed young man who appeared with his son.

This introduces a feature rather common in phantasms of the dead: some indication of happiness, something to take away any feeling of gloom or sorrow. Thus, a young man is drowned by the foundering of the La Plata telegraphic ship in December, 1874; and, just before the news arrived, his brother in London dreamed that he was at a magnificent fête, in a spacious garden with illuminated fountains and groups of gentlemen and ladies, when he met his brother in evening dress, and "the very image of buoyant health." He was surprised, and said: "Hallo! D__, how are you here?" His brother shook hands with him and said: "Did you not know I have been wrecked again?" The next morning the news of the loss of the ship was in the papers.[10] Here, whether the phantasm was caused by the dead man himself, or by some other being, it was apparently intended to show that the deceased was as cheerful and well off after death as during life.

So, when the voice of Miss Gambier Parry was heard twelve hours after her death by her former governess, Sister Bertha, at the House of Mercy, Bovey Tracey, Devonshire, it said, "in the brightest and most cheerful tone, 'I am here with you.'" And on being asked, "Who are you?" the voice replied, "You mustn't know yet."[11]

And again, when a gentleman going to the dining-room for an evening smoke, sees his sister-in-law, he says: "Maggie suddenly appeared, dressed in white, with a most heavenly expression on her face. She fixed her eyes on me, walked round the room, and disappeared through the door that leads into the garden."[12] This was the day after her death. Yet one more instance: Mr. J. G. Kenlemaus, when in Paris, was awoke one morning by the voice of a favorite little son of five years old, whom he had left quite well in London. He also saw his face in the centre of a bright opaque white mass, his eyes bright, his mouth smiling. The voice heard was that of extreme delight, such as only a happy child can utter. Yet the child had then just died.[13] Whose telepathic influence caused this phantasm of this happy, smiling child to appear to the father? Surely no living person, but rather some spirit friend or guardian wishing to show that the joyousness of life still remained with the child, though its earthly body was cold and still.

Another characteristic feature of many of these dreams

or waking phantasms is that they often occur, not at the moment of death but just before the news of the death reaches the percipient, or there is some other characteristic feature that seems especially calculated to cause a deep impression, and give a lasting conviction of spiritual existence. Several cases of this kind are given or referred to in the Proceedings of the Society for Psychical Research (Pt. XV., p , 31). A most extraordinary example is that of Mr. F. G., of Boston, then of St. Louis, Mo., who, when in St. Joseph, Mo., fully occupied with business, saw a phantasm of his only sister, who had been dead nine years. It was at noonday while he was writing, and she appeared close to him and perfectly life-like, so that for a moment he thought it was really herself, and called her by her name. He saw every detail of her dress and appearance, and particularly noticed a bright red line or scratch on the right hand side of her face. The vision so impressed him that he took the next train home, and told what he had seen to his father and mother. His father was inclined to ridicule him for his belief in its being anything supernatural, but when he mentioned the scratch on the face his mother nearly fainted, and told them with tears in her eyes, that she had herself made that scratch accidentally, after her daughter's death, but had carefully hidden it with powder, and that no living person but herself knew of it. A few weeks after, the mother died happy in her belief that she would rejoin her daughter in a better world.[14] Here we can clearly see an important purpose in the appearance of the phantasm, to give comfort to a mother about to die, in the assurance that her beloved daughter, though mourned as dead, was still alive.

A case which illustrates both of the characteristics just alluded to, is that of the Rev. C. C. Wambey of Salisbury, England, who, one Sunday evening, was walking on the downs, engaged in composing a congratulatory letter to a very dear friend so that he might have it on his birthday, when he heard a voice saying, "What, write to a dead man; write to a dead man!" No one was near him, and he tried to think it was an illusion, and went on with his composition, when again he heard the voice saying more loudly than before, "What, write to a dead man; write to a *dead* man?" He now understood the meaning of the voice, but, nevertheless, sent the letter, and in reply received the expected intelligence that his friend was dead. Surely, in this case no living agent could have produced this auditory phantasm, which was strikingly calculated to impress the recipient with the idea that his friend was, though dead as regards the earthly life, in reality very much alive, while the spice of banter in the words would tend to show that death was by no means a melancholy event to the subject of it.

In view of the examples now given of phantasms appearing for a very definite purpose, and being in most cases perfectly adapted to produce the desired effect--examples which could be very largely increased from the rich storehouse of the publications of the Society for Psychical Research-- the theory put forth by Mr. Myers,[a] that phantasms of the dead are so vague and purposeless as to suggest mere "dead men's dreams" telepathically communicated to the living, seems to me a most extraordinary one. No doubt the range of these phenomena is very great, and in some cases there may be no purpose in the appearance so far as the percipient is concerned. But these are certainly not typical or by any means the best attested or the most numerous; and it seems to me to be a proof of the weakness of the telepathic theory that almost all the cases I have adduced, and many more of like import, have been passed by almost or quite unnoticed by those who support that view.

We have one more class of evidence to notice,--that of premonitions. These are of all kinds from those announcing very trivial events, to such as foretell accidents or death. They are not so frequent as other phantasms, but some of them are thoroughly well attested, and it is difficult to avoid the conclusion that they are realities, and that they are due, generally speaking, to the same agencies as objective veridical phantasms. One or two examples may be given.

A striking case is that of Mrs. Morrison, who was living in the Province of Wellesley, Malay Peninsula, in 1878, and one morning, when awake, heard a voice distinctly say, "If there is darkness at the eleventh hour, there will be death." On starting up in bed the same words were slowly and deliberately repeated. A week afterwards her little girl was taken seriously ill, and some days later, after a week of cloudless weather, a storm came on one morning, a few minutes before eleven, and the sky became black with clouds. At one o'clock the same day the child died.[15] The unusual character of the warning renders this case a very remarkable one.

In another case, Miss R. F. Curtis, of London, dreams that she sees a lady in black who passes her, and is then seen lying on the road, with a crowd of people round her. Some think she is dead, some that she is not dead; and on asking her name, the dreamer is told she is Mrs. C__, a friend living on Clapham Common, who had not been heard of for some time. In the morning Miss Curtis tells her sister of her dream; and about a week afterwards, they hear that the day after the dream, Mrs. C__ had stumbled over a high curb-stone, and had fallen on the road very much hurt.

Still more extraordinary is the case of the Yorkshire vicar, who, when a young man of nineteen, was at Invercargill, in New Zealand, and there met a man he knew as a sailor on the ship he had come out in, and agreed to go with him and several others on an excursion to the island of Ruapuke, to stay a day or two for fishing and shooting. They were to start at four the next morning, in order to cross the bar with the high tide, and they agreed to call the vicar in time. He went to bed early with the fullest intention to go with them, and with no doubt or hesitation in his mind. The thing was settled. On his way upstairs to bed he seemed to hear a voice saying, "*Don't go with those men.*" There was no one near, but he asked, "Why not?" The voice, which seemed inside of him, said with emphasis, "You are *not* to go"; and on further question these words were repeated. Then he asked, "How can I help it? They will call me up." And, most distinctly and emphatically, the same voice said, "*You must bolt your door.*" When he got to the room, he found there was a strong bolt to the door, which he had not remembered. At first he determined he would go, as he was accustomed to take his own way at all hazards. But he felt staggered, and had a feeling of mysterious peril, and after much hesitation finally bolted the door, and went to sleep. In the morning about three he was called, the door violently shaken and kicked but though awake he did not speak, and finally the men went away cursing and shouting. About nine o'clock he went down to breakfast, and was at once asked if he had heard what had happened, and was then told that the boat with the party for Ruapuke had been upset on the bar, and *every one of them drowned.* Some of the bodies were washed up on the beach that day, and the others a day or two later, and he adds: "If I had been with them, I must have perished beyond a doubt."

Now what are we to say of this determined, warning

voice that insisted on being heard and attended to? Who and what was the being that foresaw the catastrophe that was to happen, and saved the one that it could save? Du Prel would say that it was the second self, the unconscious *ego*, that produced this inner voice; but, as we have shown, this purely hypothetical explanation is both unintelligible and inconceivable, and explains nothing, since the suggested cause has not been proved to exist, nor can it be shown how the knowledge exhibited had been acquired. But phantasms of the dead, manifesting themselves in a way to prove their identity, or exhibiting knowledge which neither the percipient nor any conceivable living agent possesses, afford strong proof that the so-called dead still live, and are able in various ways to influence their friends in earth-life. We will, therefore, briefly summarize the evidence now adduced, and see how the spiritualistic theory gives a consistent and intelligible explanation of it.

It is evident that any general theory of phantasms must deal also with the various cases of "doubles," or undoubted phantasms of the living. The few examples of apparent voluntary production of these by a living person have been supposed to prove the actual production by them, or by their unconscious *egos*; but the difficulties in the way of this view have been already pointed out. In many cases there is no exercise of will, sometimes not even a thought directed to the place or person where, or to whom, the phantasm appears;

and it is altogether irrational to ascribe the production of so marvellous an effect as, for example, a perfectly life-like phantasm of two persons, a carriage, and a horse, visible to three persons at different points of its progress through space (as described in my first article *i.e.,* _S430_), to an agent who is totally unconscious of any agency in the matter. What is termed the agent, that is the person whose "double" is produced, may be a *condition* towards the production of the phantasm without being the *cause*. I write a telegram to a friend a thousand miles away, and that friend receives my message in an hour or two. But the possibility of sending the message does not reside in me, but in a whole series of contributory agencies from the earliest inventors of the telegraph, down to the clerks who transmit and receive the message.

The clue to a true explanation of these very puzzling "doubles," as of all the other varied phenomena of phantasms and hauntings is, I believe, afforded by the following passage by one of the most thoughtful and experienced of modern spiritualists, Dr. Eugene Crowell:--

I have frequently consulted my spirit friends upon this question, and have invariably been told by them that a spirit while in mortal form cannot for an instant leave it; were it to do so, death would at once ensue; and, that the appearance of one's self at another place from that in which the body at the moment is, is simply a personation by another spirit, who thus often accomplishes a purpose desired by his mortal friend, or some other useful purpose is accomplished by the personation. I am informed, and believe, that in cases of trance, where the subjects have supposed that their spirits have left their bodies, and visited the spheres, their minds have been psychologically impressed with views representing spiritual scenes, objects, and sounds, and many times these impressions are so apparently real and truthful that the reality itself barely exceeds these representations of it, but these are all subjective impressions, not actual experiences.[16]

Accepting, then, as proved by the various classes of phantasms and the information conveyed by them, that the spirits of the so-called dead still live, and that some of them can, under special conditions, and in various ways, make their existence known to us, or influence us unconsciously to ourselves, let us see what reasonable explanation we can give of the cause and purpose of these phenomena.

In every case that passes beyond simple transference of a thought from one living person to another, it seems probable that other intelligences co-operate. There is much evidence to show that the continued association of spirits with mortals is in many cases beneficial or pleasurable to the former, and if we remember the number of very commonplace people who are daily and yearly dying around us, we shall have a sufficient explanation of those trivial and commonplace yet veridical dreams and impressions which at first sight seem so unintelligible. The production of these dreams, impressions, and phantasms, may be a pleasurable exercise of the lower spiritual faculties, as agreeable to some spirits as billiards, chemical experiments, or practical jokes are to some mortals.

Many hauntings, on the other hand, seem to show one mode of the inevitable punishment of crime in the spirit world. The criminal is drawn by remorse or by some indefinable attraction, to haunt the place of his crime, and to continually reproduce or act over some incidents connected with it. It is true that the victim appears in haunted houses, as often as the criminal, but it does not at all follow that the victim is always there, unless he or she was a participator in the crime, or continued to indulge feelings of revenge against the actual criminal.

Again, if there be a spiritual world, if those whose existence on earth has come to an end still live, what is more natural than that many spirits should be distressed at the disbelief, or doubt, or misconception, that so widely prevail, with respect to a future life, and should use whatever power they possess to convince us of our error. What more natural than that they should wish, whenever possible, to give some message to their friends, if only to assure them that death is not the end, that they still live, and are not unhappy. Many facts seem to show us that the beautiful idea of guardian spirits is not a mere dream, but a frequent, perhaps universal reality. Thus will be explained the demon of Socrates, which always warned him against danger, and the various forms of advice, information, or premonition which so many persons receive. The numerous cases in which messages are given from those recently dead, in order to do some trivial act of justice or of kindness, are surely what we should expect; while the fact that although indications are frequently given of a crime having been committed, it is but rarely that the criminal is denounced, indicates, either that the feeling of revenge does not long persist, or that earthly modes of punishment are not approved of by the denizens of the spirit world.

The powers of communication of spirits with us, and ours of receiving their communications, vary greatly. Some of us can only be influenced by ideas or impressions, which we think are altogether the product of our own minds. Others can be so strongly acted on that they feel an inexplicable emotion, leading to action beneficial to themselves or to others. In some cases, warning or information can be given through dreams, in others by waking vision. Some spirits have the power of producing visual, others audible hallucinations to certain persons. More rarely, and needing more special conditions, they can produce phantasms, which are audible or visible to all who may be present--real entities which give off light or sound waves, and thus act upon our senses like living beings or material objects. Still more rarely these phantasms are tangible as well as visual--real though temporary living forms, capable of acting like human beings, and of exerting considerable force on ordinary matter.

If we look upon these phenomena not as anything supernatural, but as the perfectly natural and orderly exercise of the faculties and powers of spiritual beings for the purpose of communicating with those still in the physical body, we shall find every objection answered, and every difficulty disappear. Nothing is more common than objections to the triviality or the partiality of the communications alleged to be from spirits. But the most trivial message or act, if such that no living person could have given or performed it, may give proof of the existence of other intelligences around us. And the partiality often displayed, one person being warned and saved, while others are left to die, is but an indication of the limited power of spirits to act upon us, combined with the limited receptivity of spirit influence on our part. In conclusion, I submit, that the brief review now given of the various classes of phantasms of the living and of the dead, demonstrates the inadequacy of all the explanations in which telepathy between living persons, or the agency of the unconscious *ego* are exclusively concerned, since these explanations are only capable of dealing with a small proportion of the cases that actually occur. Furthermore, I urge, that nothing less fundamental and far-reaching than the agency of disembodied intelligences acting in co-operation with our own powers of thought-transference and spiritual insight, can afford a rational and intelligible explanation of the whole range of the phenomena.

Notes Appearing in the Original Work
[1]Phantasms of the Living, Vol. I., p -108. on
[2]Proc. Soc. Ps. Res., Vol. I., . on
[3]Proc. Soc. Ps. Res., Vol. VI., . on
[4]Phantasms of the Living, Vol. II., . on
[5]This was Sir David Brewster's expression after witnessing Home's phenomena. See Home's "Incidents of my Life," Appendix, . on
[6]Phantasms of the Living, Vol. I., . on
[7]Proc. Soc. Ps. Res., Part VIII., p -98. on
[8]Harrison's "Spirits before our Eyes," . on
[9]Harrison's "Spirits before our Eyes," , extracted from "Glimpses of the Supernatural," by the Rev. F. G. Lee. on
[10]Proc. Soc. Ps. Res., Part XIV., . on
[11]Phantasms of the Living, Vol. I., . on
[12]Phantasms of the Living, Vol. II., . on
[13]Proc. Soc. Ps. Res., Vol. I., . on
[14]Proc. Soc. Ps. Res., Part XV., p , 18. on
[15]Proc. Soc. Ps. Res., Part XIII., . on
[16]Primitive Christianity and Modern Spiritualism, Vol. II., . on

PSYCHOGRAPHY IN THE PRESENCE OF MR. KEELER

(S452: 1892)

On January 19th, 1887, while in Washington, I accompanied some friends, two of whom were complete skeptics, to one of Mr. Keeler's seances. Before the seance commenced, it was suggested that the paper block on which messages were usually written and which was lying on a table, should be privately marked. Accordingly one of the skeptics loosened the edges of the block and marked about a dozen sheets with his initials--L. O. H. At the seance, the medium sits in front of a calico screen about five feet high hung across the corner of the room, behind which is a small table, a tambourine, stick, bell, etc. A lady from among the visitors sits beside the medium, who places both his hands upon her arm, and another calico screen tied across at the level of their necks hides the lower portion of their bodies. From behind the calico screen, above the head of the medium, a hand appears which takes a pencil and the paper block from the hand of a gentleman sitting near. The sound of writing is then heard, a sheet of paper seems to be torn off, and is immediately thrown over the screen and falls between the medium and the spectators. It is found to contain either some remark pertinent to what has been occurring at the moment or a message for some of the audience; and frequently a dozen or more such messages are given in the course of the evening, most of which are said by the recipients to contain names or facts which they recognize as correct. Sometimes a hand holding the pencil, appears to come bodily through the calico screen and writes on the paper block held by a person indicated. On this evening, I was asked to hold the block, and it was written on by a hand which appeared to come through a slit in the screen just above the medium's shoulder. The writing was rapid and partly unintelligible, but the words appear to be--"Friends were here to write, but only this one could this time. Come when they can." Later on a paper was thrown out to me containing these words--"I am here. William Wallace." Both the sheets are initialed L. O. H., showing that they could not have been prepared beforehand. No aperture could be found in the calico screen when it was examined after the seance, and no means could be discovered by which any person could have entered the corner of the room cut off by the screen. There was sufficient light to see everything and to read the writing, and full examination of the room was permitted both before and after the seance.

At another seance on February 21st, a paper was thrown out to me on which was the following message, in a different handwriting from the previous one--"I write for Mr. William Wallace, my old friend, to say that he is desirous of giving you an important message and will do so on a clear night when he can write himself. William Martin."

Two days afterward, I had another message in the same writing, beginning--"I am William Martin, and I come for Mr. William Wallace, who could not write this time after all"--and then the message goes on to refer to a matter on which I had written a letter to a newspaper that very morning. These two communications are important on account of the person from whom they purport to come. My eldest brother, William, had been educated as an architect and surveyor, and after leaving the gentleman with whom he had been articled, he went to London and engaged himself with a large London builder, to obtain a practical knowledge of materials and construction. This builder was named Martin, and he had a son about my brother's age. This was in the year 1830 or thereabouts, and when I was living with my brother some ten years later, he used often to refer to his friend Martin, but I do not remember hearing him spoken of in any other way, and therefore did not know his Christian name. Since my brother died, in 1845, I have heard nothing of these

Martins, and no one in America, besides my brother John, who resides in California, and myself, could possibly know anything of the relations existing sixty years ago between them and my brother. I do not think I have ever heard their names mentioned since my brother's death, and it was therefore most startling and altogether unexpected to have the name brought before me in this manner in connection with that of my brother. I may add that on enquiring of my sister, who being nearer my brother's age, knew more of his early life, she informs me that the Christian name of both the elder Martin and of his son was William.

At a subsequent seance on February 26th, I received a message in quite a distinct handwriting, claiming to be from the elder Martin and stating that he was a friend of my father's. Whether this was so I do not know, but as my father lived much in London in his early life, it is very probable, and will account for my brother's business connection with the Martins. The essential point, however, is, that after more than forty years of silence and forgetfulness, the names of these Martins and my brother should be brought before me at the place and in the manner here described.

Notes on the Growth of Opinion as to Obscure Psychical Phenomena During the Last Fifty Years (S478: 1893)

Having been more or less acquainted with psychical phenomena for half a century it appears to me that a few notes of opinion I have witnessed during that period may not be uninteresting to the Congress. I must apologise for the brief and fragmentary nature of the communication, having neither time nor materials for a more detailed statement.

It was about the year 1843 that I first became interested in psychical phenomena owing to the violent discussion then going on as to the reality of the painless surgical operations performed by Dr. Elliotson and other English surgeons on patients in the mesmeric trance. The greatest surgical and psychological authorities of the day declared that the patients were either impostors or persons naturally insensible to pain; the operating surgeons were accused of bribing their patients; and Dr. Elliotson was accused of "polluting the temple of science." The Medico Chirurgical Society opposed the reading of a paper describing an amputation during the magnetic trance, while Dr. Elliotson himself was ejected from his professorship in the University of London. It was at this time generally believed that all the now well-known phenomena of hypnotism were the result of imposture.

It so happened that in the year 1844 I heard an able

lecture on mesmerism by Mr. Spencer Hall, and the lecturer assured his audience that most healthy persons could mesmerise some of their friends, and reproduce many of the phenomena he had shown on the platform. This led me to try for myself, and I soon found that I could mesmerise with varying degrees of success, and before long I succeeded in producing in my own room, either alone with my patient or in the presence of friends, most of the usual phenomena. Partial or complete catalepsy, paralysis of the motor nerves, in certain directions, or of any special sense, every kind of delusion produced by suggestion, insensibility to pain, and community of sensation with myself when at a considerable distance from the patient, were all demonstrated, in such a number of patients and under such varied conditions as to satisfy me of the genuiness of the phenomena. I thus learnt my first great lesson in the inquiry into these obscure fields of knowledge, never to accept the disbelief of great men or their accusations of imposture or of imbecility, as of any weight when opposed to the repeated observation of facts by other men, admittedly sane and honest. The whole history of science shows us that whenever the educated and scientific men of any age have denied the facts of other investigators on *a priori* grounds of absurdity or impossibility, the deniers have always been wrong.

A few years later, and all the more familiar facts of mesmerism were accepted by medical men, and explained more or less satisfactorily to themselves, as not being essentially different from known diseases of the nervous system; and of late years the more remarkable phenomena, including clairvoyance both as to facts known and those unknown to the mesmeriser, have been established as absolute realities.

Next we come to the researches of Baron von Reichenbach on the action of magnets and crystals upon sensitives. I well remember how these were scouted by the late Dr. W. B. Carpenter and by Professor Tyndall, and how I was pitied for my credulity in accepting them. But many of his results have now been tested by French and English observers and have been found to be correct.

Then we all remember how the phenomena of the stigmata, which have occurred at many epochs in the Catholic church, were always looked upon by sceptics as gross imposture and the believers in its reality as too far gone in credulity to be seriously reasoned with. Yet when the case of Louise Lateau was thoroughly investigated by sceptical physicians and could be no longer doubted, the facts were admitted, and when, later on, somewhat similar appearances were produced in hypnotic patients by suggestion, the whole matter was held to be explained.

Second-sight, crystal-seeing, automatic writing, and allied phenomena have been usually treated either as self-delusion or as imposture, but now that they have been carefully studied by Mr. Myers, Mr. Stead, and other enquirers, they have been found to be genuine facts; and it has been further proved that they often give information not known to any one present at the time, and even sometimes predict future events with accuracy.

Trance mediums who give similar information to that obtained through crystal seeing or automatic writing, have long been held up to scorn as impostors of the grossest kind. They have been the butt of newspaper writers, and have been punished for obtaining money under false pretences; yet when one of these trance mediums, the well-known Mrs. Piper, was subject to a stringent examination by some of the acutest members of the Society for Psychical Research, the unanimous testimony was that there was no imposture in the case, and that, however the knowledge exhibited was acquired, Mrs. Piper herself could never have acquired it through the medium of her ordinary senses.

Nothing has been more constantly disbelieved and ridiculed than the alleged appearance of phantasms of the living or of the recently dead, whether seen by one person alone, or by several together. Imagination, disease, imposture, or erroneous observation have been again and again put forth as sufficient explanation of these appearances. But when carefully examined they do not prove to be impostures, but stand out with greater distinctness as veridical and sometimes objective phenomena, as is sufficiently proved by the mass of well attested and well sifted evidence published by the Society for Psychical Research. Still more subject to ridicule and contempt are ghosts and haunted houses. It has been said that these disappeared with the advent of gas; but so far from this being the case there is ample testimony at the present day to phenomena which come under these categories.

In this connection also we have not merely appearances, which may be explained away as collective hallucinations, but actual physical phenomena of such a material character as stone-throwing, bell-ringing, movements of furniture, independent writing and drawing, and many other manifestations of force guided by intelligence which is yet not the force or the intelligence of those present. Records of such phenomena pervade history, and during the last century and especially during the last half century, they have been increasingly prevalent, and have been supported by the same kind and the same amount of cumulative testimony as all the preceding classes of phenomena. Some of these cases are now being investigated, and there is no sign of their being traced to imposture. From personal knowledge and careful experiments I can testify that some of these physical phenomena are realities, and I cannot doubt that the fullest investigation will result, as in all the other cases, in their recognition as facts which any comprehensive theory must recognise and explain.

What are termed spirit photographs, the appearance on a photographic plate of other figures besides those of the sitters, often those of deceased friends of the sitters, have now been known for more than twenty years. Many competent observers have tried experiments successfully; but the facts seemed too extraordinary to carry conviction to any but the experimenters themselves, and any allusion to the subject has usually been met with a smile of incredulity or a confident assertion of imposture. It mattered not that most of the witnesses were experienced photographers who took precautions which rendered it absolutely impossible that they were imposed upon. The most incredible suppositions were put forth by those who only had ignorance and incredulity to qualify them as judges, in order to show that deception was possible. And now we have another competent witness, Mr. Traill Taylor, for many years editor of the *British Journal of Photography*, who, taking every precaution that his life-long experience could suggest, yet obtained on his plates figures which, so far as normal photography is concerned, ought not to have been there.

Lastly, we come to consider the claim of the intelligences who are connected with most of these varied phenomena to be the spirits of deceased men and women, such claim being supported by tests of various kinds, especially by giving accurate information regarding themselves as to facts totally unknown to the medium or to any person present. Records of such tests are numerous in spiritual literature as well as in the publications of the Society for Psychical Research, but at present they are regarded as inconclusive, and various theories of a double or multiple personality, of a subconscious or second self, or of a lower stratum of consciousness are called in to explain them or to attempt to explain them. The stupendous difficulty that, if these phenomena and these tests are to be all attributed to the "second self" of living persons, then that second self is almost always a deceiving and a lying self, however moral and truthful the visible and tangible first self may be, has, so far as I know, never been rationally explained; yet this cumbrous and unintelligible hypothesis finds great favour with those who have always been accustomed to regard the belief in a spirit world, and more particularly a belief that the spirits of our dead friends can and do sometimes communicate with us, as unscientific, unphilosophical, and superstitious. Why it should be unscientific, more than any other hypothesis which alone serves to explain intelligibly a great body of facts, has never been explained. The antagonism which it excites seems to be mainly due to the fact that it is, and has long been in some form or other, the belief of the religious world and of the ignorant and superstitious of all ages, while a total disbelief in spiritual existence has been the distinctive badge of modern scientific scepticism. But we find that the belief of the uneducated and unscientific multitude rested on a broad basis of facts which the scientific world scouted and scoffed at as absurd and impossible. Now, however, we are discovering, as this brief sketch has shown, that the alleged facts are one after another proved to be real facts, and, strange to say, with little or no exaggeration, since almost every one of them, though implying abnormal powers in human being or the agency of a spirit-world around us, has been strictly paralleled in the present day, and has been subjected to the close scrutiny of the scientific and sceptical with little or no modification of their essential nature. Since, then, the scientific world has been proved to have been totally wrong in its denial of the facts, as being contrary to laws of nature and therefore incredible, it seems highly probable, *a priori*, it may have been equally wrong as to the spirit hypothesis, the dislike of which mainly led to their disbelief in the facts. For myself, I never have been able to see why any one hypothesis should be less scientific than another, except so far as one explains the whole of the facts and the other explains only a part of them. It was this alone that rendered the theory of gravitation more scientific than that of cycles and epicycles, the undulatory theory of light more scientific than the emission theory, and the theory of Darwin more scientific than that of Lamarck. It is often said that we must exhaust known causes before we call in unknown causes to explain phenomena. This may be admitted, but I cannot see how it applies to the present question. The "second" or "sub-conscious self" with its wide stores of knowledge how gained no one knows, its distinct character, its low morality, its constant lies, is as purely a theoretical cause as is the spirit of a deceased person or any other spirit. It can in no sense be termed "a known cause." To call this hypothesis "scientific," and that of spirit agency "unscientific" is to beg the question at issue. That theory is most scientific which best explains the whole series of phenomena; and I therefore claim that the spirit-hypothesis is the most scientific, since even those who oppose it most strenuously often admit that it does explain all the facts, which cannot be said of any other hypothesis. This very brief and very imperfect sketch of the progress of opinion on the questions this Congress has met to discuss leads us, I think, to some valuable and reassuring conclusions. We are taught, first, that human nature is not so wholly and utterly the slave of delusion as has sometimes been alleged, since almost every alleged superstition is now shown to have had a basis of fact. Secondly, those who believe, as I do, that spiritual beings can and do, subject to general laws and for certain purposes, communicate with us, and even produce material effects in the world around us, must see in the steady advance of inquiry and of interest in these questions, the assurance that, so far as their beliefs are logical deductions from the phenomena they have witnessed, those beliefs will at no distant date be accepted by all truth-seeking inquirers.

A Collection of Essays on Spiritualism

Parkstone, Dorset, England.

SPIRITUALISM AND SOCIAL DUTY

(S545: 1898)

Friends and Fellow Spiritualists,--For the last ten years my attention has been given to other subjects than Spiritualism; and less than three years ago, in a new edition of my writings on the subject,[1] I have restated my firm conviction as to the reality and importance of our inquiry and the worthlessness of all the arguments of our opponents. I have, therefore, nothing whatever to say to you as to Spiritualism itself. But I will take the present opportunity of laying before you a few observations on what appears to me to be the relation of the beliefs we hold as Spiritualists to that subject which now mainly occupies my thoughts--how to raise the bulk of our people out of that terrible slough of destitution, grinding life-long labour for bare subsistence, and shortened lives, uncheered by any of those refinements of art or enjoyment of Nature which are essential to the development of what is best in humanity. In a work published a few weeks since,[2] I have given ample proof that such is, to-day, the condition of a large proportion of our people, notwithstanding an increase of wealth and of wealth-creating power unequalled in the history of the world, and adequate, if properly utilised, to give not only abundance of all necessaries, but comforts, luxuries, and ample leisure to all. On these matters, however, I will now say no more, but will ask your attention to a few remarks on what I consider to be the relation of Spiritualism to Social Duty.

The old doctrine as to the nature of the future life was based upon the idea of rewards and punishments, which were supposed to be dependent upon *dogmatic beliefs* and ceremonial *observances*. The atheist, the agnostic, even the Unitarian, were for centuries held to be certain of future punishment; and, with the unbaptised infant, the Sabbath-breaker, and the abstainer from church-going, were alike condemned to hell-fire. Beliefs and observances were then held to be of the first importance; disposition, conduct, health, and happiness were of no account.

The new doctrines--founded almost wholly on the teachings of Modern Spiritualism, though now widely accepted, even among non-Spiritualists--are the very reverse of all this. They are based upon the conception of mental and moral continuity; that there are no imposed punishments; that dogmatic beliefs are absolutely unimportant, except so far as they affect our relations with our fellows; and that forms and ceremonies, and the complex observances of most religions, are equally unimportant. On the other hand, what are of the most vital importance are motives, with the actions that result from them, and everything that develops and exercises the whole mental, moral, and physical nature, resulting in happy and healthy lives for every human being. The future life will be simply a continuation of the present, under new conditions; and its happiness or misery will be dependent upon how we have developed all that is best in our nature here.

Under the old theory the soul could be saved by a mere change of beliefs and the performance of certain ceremonial observances. The body was nothing; happiness was nothing; pleasure was often held to be a sin; hence any amount of punishment, torture, and even death were considered justifiable in order to produce this change and save the soul.

On the new theory it is the body that develops, and to some extent saves, the soul. Disease, pain, and all that shortens and impoverishes life, are injurious to the soul as well as to the body. Not only is a healthy body necessary for a sound mind, but equally so for a fully-developed soul--a soul that is best fitted to commence its new era of development in the spirit world. Inasmuch as we have fully utilised and developed all our faculties--bodily, mental, and spiritual--and have done all in our power to aid others in a similar development, so have we prepared future well-being for ourselves and for them.

All this is the common knowledge and belief of Spiritualists; and I should not have thought it necessary to restate it, were it not that our creed is often misunderstood and misrepresented by outsiders, and also because it is preliminary to certain conclusions which, I think, logically follow from it, but which are not so generally accepted among us.

It seems to me that, holding these beliefs as to the future life and what is the proper and only preparation for it, we Spiritualists must feel ourselves bound to work strenuously for such improved social conditions as may render it possible for all to live a full and happy life, for *all* to develop and utilise the various faculties they possess, and thus be prepared to enter at once on the progressive higher life of the spirit-world. We *know* that a life of continuous and grinding bodily labour, in order to obtain a bare existence; a life almost necessarily devoid of beauty, of refinement, of communion with Nature; a life without adequate relaxation, and with no opportunity for the higher culture; a life full of temptation and with no cheering hope of a happy and peaceful old age, is as bad for the welfare of the soul as it is for that of the body.

If the accounts we get of the spirit world have any truth in them, the reclamation and education of the millions of undeveloped or degraded spirits which annually quit this earth, is a sore burden, a source of trouble and sorrow to those more advanced spirits who have charge of them. This burden must, for a long time to come at all events, *necessarily* be great, on account of the numbers of the less advanced races and peoples still upon the earth; but that *we*, who call ourselves *civilised*, who have learnt so much of the secret powers and mysteries of the universe, who by means of those powers could easily provide a decent and rational and happy life for our whole population--that *we* should send to the spirit world, day by day and year by year, millions of men and women, of children, and of infants, all sent there before their time through want of the necessary means of a healthy life, or by the various diseases and accidents forced upon them by the vile conditions under which alone we give them the opportunity of living at all--this is a disgrace and a crime!

I firmly believe--and the fact is supported by abundant evidence--that the very poorest class of our great cities, those that live constantly below the margin of poverty, who are without the comforts, the necessaries, and even the decencies of life, are, nevertheless, as a class, quite as good morally, and often as high intellectually, as the middle and upper classes who look down upon them as in every way their inferiors. Their condition, socially and morally, is the work of society; and in so far as they appear worse than others they are made so by society. What should we ourselves have been if we had had no education, no repose, no refined or decent homes, no means of cleanliness, which is not only next to, but is a source of, godliness; surrounded by every kind of temptation, and not unfrequently forced into crime? And a direct consequence of the millions who are compelled to lead such lives are the millions of infants who die prematurely--a slaughter a thousand times worse than that of Herod, going on year by year in our midst; surely their innocent blood cries out against our rulers, against all of *us*, who choose such rulers; and more especially against us Spiritualists, who know the higher law, if we do not work with all our strength for a radical reform.

As many of my friends here know, I myself, against all my early prepossessions, have come to believe that some form of Socialism is the only complete remedy for this state of things; and I define Socialism as simply the organisation of labour for the highest common good. Just as the Post Office is organised labour in one department for the benefit of all alike; just as the railways might be organised as a whole for the benefit of the community; just as numbers of vast industries are organised, more especially in America, for the exclusive benefit of rings of capitalists--so all necessary and useful labour might be organised for the benefit of all.

I ask you to think over this question; and above all things, I ask you to consider the necessity for real and fundamental remedies, not mere palliatives, which have been tried with ever-increasing energy and good-will throughout the century, and have absolutely failed. The evil has grown, just as if no such remedies had been applied at all. Charity has increased enormously, and has failed. Now it is time for us to try Justice.

A few years since a talented writer[3] used, and at once popularised, a new term--'equality of opportunity.' It expresses briefly and forcibly what may be termed the minimum of social justice. The same idea had been urged by other writers, especially by Herbert Spencer in his volume on 'Justice,' when he declared that justice requires every man to receive 'the results of his own nature and consequent actions'--this and this only. Fundamentally, the two ideas are the same, but 'equality of opportunity' is the more simple and intelligible expression of it.

To Spiritualists, who realise that every child born into this world is a living soul, come here to prepare itself for the higher life of the spirit world, it must appear a crime against that world and against humanity not to see that every such child has the best possible nurture and training, at the very least till it arrives at the adult age and becomes an independent unit of the social organism. And if to each is due the best, then none can have more than the best, and we come thus again to EQUALITY OF OPPORTUNITY.

Of course, many of you will say, 'This is impossible. How can we possibly give this equality of nurture and education to every child?' I admit that it is difficult--by no means impossible. It must, of course, be brought about gradually; and where there is a will there is a way. As Herbert Spencer said of another matter--the nationalisation of the land--'justice sternly demands that it be done;' and if we, boasting of our civilisation, declare that it cannot be done, then so much the worse for us and for our false civilisation. But it wants only the will. And it is our duty, as Spiritualists, to help to create that will.

But again, you will say, 'Where are the means of doing this? We are already taxed as much as we can bear.' True, we are shamefully over-taxed, but, instead of increasing the taxes, there is a necessary corollary of 'equality of opportunity' which will not only give us ample funds to bring it about, but will at the same time greatly reduce taxation and ultimately abolish it altogether. For, if every child is given equality of opportunity, and every man and woman receives only 'the results of their own nature and consequent actions,' then it is evident that there must be no *inequality* of inheritance; and to give equality of inheritance, the State, that is, the community, must be the universal inheritor of all wealth. At first, of course, it would only be needful to take surplus wealth above a fixed maximum; and, so far from this being an injury to the heirs of a millionaire, it would be a great benefit; for it is admitted that nothing has so demoralising an effect on the young as the certainty of inheriting great wealth; and examples of this come before us every year and almost every month. This is the real teaching of the parable of Dives and Lazarus; this gives us the true meaning of Christ's saying that a rich man shall hardly enter into the kingdom of heaven.

Now, many who dislike the idea of Socialism--chiefly, I think, through not understanding what it really implies--will perhaps look more favourably on this great principle of 'equality of opportunity,' since it would leave individualism untouched, would in fact render it far more complete and effective than it is now. For our present state of society is *not* true individualism, because the inequalities of opportunity in early life are so great that often the worst are forced to the top, while many of the best struggle throughout life without a chance of using their highest faculties, or developing the best part of their nature. Even Tennyson, whose mind was of an aristocratic bent, could say--

> Plowmen, shepherds, have I found, and more than once, and still could find,
> Sons of God and kings of men in utter nobleness of mind;
> Truthful, trustful, looking upward to the practised hustings-liar;
> So the Higher wields the Lower, while the Lower *is* the Higher.

Here and there a cotter's babe is royal-born by
right divine;
Here and there my lord is lower than his oxen or
his swine.

Equality of opportunity would put all this right; everyone
would be able to show what power for good he possessed, and
society would be enormously benefited in consequence. At
the same time, there would be all the stimulus to be derived
from individual effort. The man who could surpass his fellows
under such equal and fair conditions would be truly great.
Some would achieve honour, some would acquire wealth;
but it would be all due to their own 'nature and consequent
actions,' and neither the honour nor the wealth would be
handed on to individuals who might not be worthy of the
one or be able to acquire the other.

I believe myself that such a perfectly fair competition,
in which all started on equal terms socially, would be an
admirable training, and would be sure to lead, ultimately, to
a voluntary co-operation and organisation of labour which
would produce most of the best results of Socialism itself.
But whether it would or not, I claim that it embodies a
great and true principle--Social Justice; and that it affords
the only non-socialistic escape from the horrible social
quagmire in which we find ourselves. As Spiritualists we
must uphold justice; and equality of opportunity for all is

but bare justice. Knowing that the life here is the school for the development of the spirit, we must feel it our duty to see that the nascent spirit in each infant has the fullest and freest opportunity of developing all its faculties and powers under the best conditions we can provide for it. And I have ventured to bring this subject before you because it is the one hope nearest to my heart; and I am sure that if the great and rapidly-increasing body of Spiritualists can be brought to consider it, and to feel that the misery and degradation around them *must* be and *can* be got rid of, and that it is especially *their* business and *their* duty to help to get rid of it, the great work will soon be taken in hand.

What we want, above all things, is to educate the people and create a public opinion adequate for the work. In this movement for justice and right, Spiritualists should take the lead, because they, more than any other body, know its vital importance both for this world and the next. The various religious sects are all working, according to their lights, in the social field; but their forces are almost exclusively directed to the alleviation of individual cases of want and misery by means of charity in various forms. But this method has utterly failed even to diminish the mass of human misery everywhere around us, because it deals with symptoms only and leaves the causes untouched. I would not say a word against even this form of charity, for those who see no higher law; but we want more of the true charity of St. Paul--the charity that thinketh no evil, that suffereth long and is kind, that rejoiceth in the truth--not only the lesser and easier charity which feeds the poor out of its superfluity, an action which St. Paul does not allow to be charity at all.

But let us Spiritualists take higher ground. Let us demand Social Justice. This will be a work worthy of our cause, to which it will give dignity and importance. It will show our fellow-countrymen that we are not mere seekers after signs and wonders, mere interviewers of the lower denizens of the spirit-world; but that our faith, founded on knowledge, has a direct influence on our lives; that it teaches us to work strenuously for the elevation and permanent well-being of all our fellow men. In order to do this our watchword must be--NOT CHARITY ONLY BUT JUSTICE.

www.ingramcontent.com/pod-product-compliance
Lightning Source LLC
Chambersburg PA
CBHW020528270326
41927CB00006B/491